U.S. Mint

Miscellaneous Letters Received from 1897 to 1903

Vol. 5

U.S. Mint

Miscellaneous Letters Received from 1897 to 1903
Vol. 5

ISBN/EAN: 9783337817220

Printed in Europe, USA, Canada, Australia, Japan

Cover: Foto ©Suzi / pixelio.de

More available books at **www.hansebooks.com**

RG 104, 8KRA-104-84-042
Box 3, Volume V

Miscellaneous Letters Received, 1897-1903.
Letters Received Relating   to the Construction
of the New Denver Mint, 1897-1906.

Supervising Architect

Supervising Architect.

JOHN A. McINTYRE,
GENERAL CONTRACTOR.
OMN 402-404 COOPER BUILDING,
DENVER, COLO.
Telephone 1238.

OWNER AND OPERATOR
ARKINS GRANITE QUARRIES.

Denver, Colo., April 30, 1901.

Leo Ullery, Esq.,

    Supt. of Construction

      U. S. Mint (New),

        Denver, Colo.

Dear Sir:-

    Replying to our conversation, relative to wire received by me from the Department, April 30, 1901, I have the honor to hand you herewith copy of letter to The Standard Granite Company this day forwarded to them, and to request that you forward said copy to the Department, with such explanation of my action as you may see fit to give, requesting that you assure the Department of my good faith and intentions in the matter. I remain,

          Very respectfully yours,

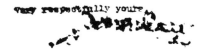

Denver,Colo., April 30th,1901

C.J.Hall, Pres.,
    Standard Granite Company,
       Hall Quarry, Maine.

Sir:-

      Your letter of April 25th,informing me of the impossibility of getting out the duplicate stone required to complete the top member of the cornice of the United States Mint building,in this city, before the middle of May, has fortunately remained unanswered.

      I this day received a telegram from the Treasury Department at Washington, advising me as follows: "You must supply stone for Mint as required by Superintendent Ullery. No further delay will be tolerated. J.K.Taylor,Supervising Architect".

      Upon the receipt of the above telegram, I immediately applied to Mr.Ullery for such information as was in his possession,to explain the purport of the Government's demand,their telegram being a great surprise to me,as I had been led to believe that the stone therein referred to was being quarried by you for immediate shipment.

      February 27th,your Mr.Clark advised me as follows: "Reply-"ing to your letter of February 25th, I would say that I have orders "from the Home Office as to the four stones to replace those con-"demned by the Superintendent,but have not as yet heard when I can "expect to receive them. Will advise you of the date and assure you "that the utmost dispatch will be used.
                     Very respectfully,
                       G.W.Clark,
                       For Standard Granite Company"

      From letters shown me by Mr.Ullery,Superintendent of Construction, I am convinced that instead of endeavoring to secure the stone called for,you have devoted your attention to an endeavor to convince the Government that you have been ill-used by the Supervising Architect and his representatives,and that the condemnation of the four stone mentioned was unnecessary and uncalled for. This action you have taken without my knowledge and consent in any way,and have seriously retarded the work and very much embarrassed me in my position with the Department.

      I now desire to advise you very positively,that no further delay on your part will be tolerated in any way. You must at once furnish the four stone called for to complete your contract in the way and manner demanded by the Government.

      As to the $750.00 approximate amount due you on the comple-

tion of your contract, I desire to say that no further amounts of any
kind will be paid, nor will any of your drafts be honored for any
amount,until the stone required to complete your contract has been
shipped,received and accepted by the Government at this point. And
I wish further to advise you that should any further delay exist in
the furnishing of this stone, I shall take measures to declare your
contract cancelled,buy the stone necessary to complete your contract,
in the open market, and commence suit against your firm for any damages resulting to me from you actions.
   I remain,
          Very respectfully yours,
           (Signed) J.A.McIntyre,
               Trux.

DENVER. P.O. & CT.H.

B

TREASURY DEPARTMENT

OFFICE OF THE SUPERVISING ARCHITECT

Washington,   April 16, 1901.

Enclosure.

Superintendent of Construction,

    U. S. Mint (new),

        Denver, Colorado.

Sir:

      There are enclosed herewith copies of letters (two) of the
12th instant from the Custodian of the Post Office and Court House
in your city, relative to the condition of the roof of that building and the necessity for outside painting, new storm doors, etc.

      You are requested to confer with the Custodian and to make a
thorough examination of the building on the line suggested by him
and to prepare specification in detail for all necessary repairs.

      Please give the roof matter your particular attention and
submit a further report as to the results attained by the method
of patching suggested by this office in a letter dated March 24,
1900, which will be found on the Custodian's files.

            Respectfully,

               Supervising Architect.

COPY.

. Office of Custodian,

U. S.

. Denver, Colo., April 12, 1901

To the Honorable,

The Secretary of the Treasury,

Washington, D. C.

Sir:

I have the honor to report, that the outside wood work of
this building is badly in need of paint, especially the outside
doors in the dome, and window casings of the upper floors, in
which places the paint is almost entirely gone.

Attention is also invited to the fact that the hinges of the
inside swinging doors on the Arapahoe street side, are badly worn
and the doors sag so that they strike.   In connection with this
I beg to state, that this building is badly in need of a system
of storm doors and I, therefore, most respectfully recommend that
instead of repairing the present swinging doors, that I be authorized to request Mr. Lee Ullery, Supt. of Construction of the new
Mint Building in this city, to give his opinion in regard to es-
tablishing a system of storm doors.

Most respectfully submitted,

(Signed)   F. P. Valentine,

Acting Custodian.

COPY.

Denver, Colo., April 12,1901

To the Honorable,

    The Secretary of the Treasury,

       Washington, D. C.

Sir:

    Referring to Department letter of March 24, 1900, "S" relative to keeping the roof of this building in repair, I have to honor to state, that the formula mentioned therein has been given a very fair trial and I am now prepared to state, that I believe this country too dry for this preparation to be successfully used, and the roof now needs a thorough overhauling and a number of places resoldered. It is, therefore, requested that I be authorized to accept proposals for placing the roof in repair with a guarantee for, at least, one year.

              Most respectfully,

       (Signed)   E. P. Valentine,

                  Acting Custodian.

Supervising Architect.

TREASURY DEPARTMENT

OFFICE OF THE SECRETARY

Washington,   May 2, 1901.

The Superintendent of Construction, U. S. Mint,

      Denver, Colorado.

Sir:

     Referring to your letter of the 18th ultimo, addressed
to the Supervising Architect, Treasury Department, and referred
to this Division, you are informed that one National Ensign,
5-1/4 x 10 feet, for use of the temporary office at the U. S.
Mint, at Denver, Colorado, has been forwarded by today's mail to
your address.

     You are requested to acknowledge the receipt of same.

     Respectfully,

                       Captain, R.C.S.,
                        Chief of Division.

Denver,Colo., May 7th,1901

Lee Ullery,Esq.,

      Superintendent of Construction,

         Denver, Colorado.

Dear Sir:-

      I have the honor to hand you herewith sketch of method suggested by Terra Cotta men for girder covering.

      This sketch was only handed to me this   day ,and I assure you the delay in securing same was in no manner my fault.

          Very respectfully,

             (Signed) J.A.McIntyre

                 T.

U. S. DEPARTMENT OF AGRICULTURE,

Climate and Crop Service of the Weather Bureau.

COLORADO SECTION.

F. H. BRANDENBURG,
LOCAL FORECAST OFFICIAL AND
SECTION DIRECTOR.

POST OFFICE BUILDING, DENVER,   May 9th 1901.

Mr. Lee Ullery,

     Supt. of Construction, U. S. Mint,

          Denver, Colorado.

Dear Sir:

       Find enclosed copy of temperature data (October 13th to

November 1st 1900, inclusive) as per your request dated May 8, 1901.

            Very truly yours,

            L. F. O. & Section Director.

Station: DENVER, COLO.

Data _Minimum temperature_

190 .	January.	February.	March.	April.	May.	June.	July.	August.	September.	October.	November.	December.	
1													
2													
3													
4													
5													
6													
7													
8													
9													
10													
11													
12													
13	43												
14	46												
15	46												
16	45												
17	38												
18	40												
19	48												
20	43												
21	30												
22	46												
23	43												
24	35												
25	34												
26	35												
27	42												
28	35												
29	36												
30	27												
31	19												
SUMS.	31												
MEANS.													

1900
ct

L. F. O. & Section Director.

MAY 15, 0. 1901

Form No. 175.
Ed. 8 22 1901 6,000.

Treasury Department,

Office of the SUPERVISING ARCHITECT,

Washington, D. C.,   May 10, 1901.

Sir:

    The receipt this day is hereby acknowledged of your communication of May 7, 1901, relative to fireproofing girders

in connection with the building under your charge,

and referring thereto you are informed that the matter will receive due consideration, and action will be taken at the earliest date.

             Respectfully,

                          J. K. TAYLOR,
                        Supervising Architect.

POSTAL TELEGRAPH-CABLE COMPANY IN CONNECTION WITH THE COMMERCIAL CABLE COMPANY.

JOHN W. MACKAY, President.
J. O. STEVENS, Sec'y.   WM. H. BAKER. V. P. & G. M.

JOHN W. MACKAY, President.
ALBERT BECK, Sec'y.   GEO. G. WARD. V. P. & G. M.

TELEGRAM 424

The Postal Telegraph-Cable Company transmits and delivers this message subject to the terms and conditions printed on the back of this blank.

Received at Main Office, 920, 17th Street, Ernest & Cranmer Building, Denver. (Telephone 1490.)

117-Ex. Ca. Wx. 43-Paid Govt

Washington, D.C., May 18th

Sup't Ullery, Mint, Denver, Colo.

Proposal being considered for Cheyenne superstructure of iron mountain
(Wyoming) stone. Do you know it's reputation where used. If not you
will be sent to quarry and adjacent points to inquire answer. quick

J. K. Taylor, Supervisor Architect.

1227P

DENVER,COLORADO: NEW MINT

TREASURY DEPARTMENT

OFFICE OF THE SUPERVISING ARCHITECT

Washington,   May 20,1901.

The Superintendent of Construction,

United States (new) Mint,

Denver, Colorado.

Sir:

In reply to your communication of the 15th
instant relative to the water submitted for analysis in connection with the supply for the
building under your charge, I have to state that
both of the samples forwarded were duly received
and the express charges thereon will be paid at
this office. You need therefore take no further
action in the matter.

Respectfully,

Acting Supervising Architect.

R.

Form 32.
Ed.12-29-'94—2,000.}

Treasury Department,

OFFICE OF THE SUPERVISING ARCHITECT,

Washington, D. C.,   May 20, 1901.

Mr. Lee Ullery,

Supt. U. S. Mint Building,

Denver, Colorado.

Sir:

I have to acknowledge the receipt of your "Estimate of Funds" required for the work on the building under your superintendence during May, 1901, 188x , *and to advise you that, as it appears the remittance of funds heretofore made to the Disbursing Agent on account of the appropriation for the building is sufficient to meet all vouchers issued or to be issued for expenditures on account of the work on the building, to and including the last day of the current month, no further remittance will be made to him at present.*

Respectfully, yours,

Jas. A. Wetmore

Acting   *Chief Executive Officer.*

F.D.

TREASURY DEPARTMENT

OFFICE OF THE SECRETARY

Washington,   May 23, 1901.

Mr. Lee Ullery,

    Superintendent of Construction of Public Buildings,

        U. S. Mint (new), Denver, Colorado.

Sir:

    I have to inform you that the Department has this day rein-
stated Mr. Benjamin Tuthill as Watchman in connection with the
building under your superintendency, to take effect from date of
oath, with compensation at the rate of $840 per annum, payable
from the appropriation for- "U. S. Mint, Denver, Colorado."

    You are authorized to issue and certify vouchers for his ser-
vices accordingly.

        Respectfully,

              Acting Secretary.

T.

DENVER. NEW MINT.

In replying to this Letter the
initials in upper right-hand
corner must be referred to.

ENCLOSURE 1507.

TREASURY DEPARTMENT

OFFICE OF THE SUPERVISING ARCHITECT

Washington,   May 24, 1901.

S

The Superintendent of Construction,

U. S. Mint (New),

Denver, Colorado.

Sir:

Find enclosed Department letter of yesterday, addressed to
Mr. Benjamin Tuthill, Denver, Col., reinstating him to the position of watchman in connection with the construction of the
building under your charge.   Please hand the letter, with the
enclosed blank oath of office, to Mr. Tuthill, directing him to
return the latter to you when properly executed, and you will
please forward it to this Department without delay.

The appointment of a watchman must not be construed as reliev-
ing the contractors of any responsibility in regard to the care
of material.

Respectfully,

James Knox Taylor

Acting Supervising Architect.

DENVER,COLO.,NEW MINT.

In replying to this Letter the
initials in upper right-hand
corner must be referred to.

TREASURY DEPARTMENT

OFFICE OF THE SUPERVISING ARCHITECT

Washington, May 24, 1901.

Superintendent of Construction,
   New Mint Building,
      Denver, Colorado.

Sir:

 I have to acknowledge the receipt of your letter of the
20th instant, in which it is suggested that considerable time
may be saved by substituting 8" terra cotta arches in deck
roof in lieu of 9" and 6" arches required by the contract of
John A. McIntyre, and you are requested to obtain a proposal
for making the above mentioned change, without cost to the
Government, and forward it to this office as soon as possible
with your definite recommendation.

     Respectfully,

          Acting Supervising Architect.

CHEYENNE.

MGD

INCLOSURE 1501.

TREASURY DEPARTMENT

OFFICE OF THE SECRETARY

Washington,   May 20, 1901.

Mr. Lee Ullery,

    Superintendent of Construction,

        U. S. Mint (New), Denver, Colorado.

Sir:

    Referring to telegram addressed to you on the 18th instant by the Supervising Architect of this Department, and to your reply by wire the same day, in regard to stone from quarries at Iron Mountain, Wyo., now being considered in connection with proposals received for the erection of the superstructure, etc., of the U. S. Post Office building, Cheyenne, Wyo., you are now more fully advised and directed in regard thereto.

    Proposals have recently been opened at the office of the Supervising Architect of this Department for the erection of the superstructure, etc., of the building named, the lowest bid being that of Messrs. Forster & Smith, Minneapolis, Minn., being alternative for the use of sandstone with granite, in the sum of one hundred and eighty-four thousand, seven hundred and thirty-seven dollars ($184,737), or of limestone with granite in the sum of one hundred and eighty-seven thousand, seven hundred and thirty-seven dollars ($187,737).   The name of the sandstone quarry is given as Rawlins, Wyo., and of the limestone quarry as Iron Mountain, Wyo.   The sample of Rawlins sandstone did not indicate satisfactory material, and it is desired to give consideration to the selection of some other material falling within the bid.   The other materials may be sandstone or limestone from the quarries at Iron Mountain, Wyo., and you are requested, therefore, to visit the quarries named, and to gather full information as to their development and capacity, and as to whether they are in such condition that they could be readily worked and satisfactory stone secured therefrom in character and sizes required.

For your information in this connection find herewith a brief schedule of the larger size stones which will be required, as shown by drawings.

You are authorized, also, in going to or coming from Iron Mountain, to visit Cheyenne, Wyo., and gather information as to whether any of the stones forming the subject of this communication is in use in that city, how long it has been in use, and what the results are as to weathering.   It has been intimated that the Rawlins sandstone has been used in the Cheyenne Capitol with unsatisfactory results, and that Iron Mountain white sandstone is being used in the erection of the Carnegie Library Building.

Mr. R. W. Bradley, general contractor, with offices at 17th Street and Capitol Avenue, Cheyenne, has intimated that he will furnish any information which may be asked in regard to the material, and, should you desire, you may call upon him and avail yourself of his offer.

Please start as early as possible, consistent with your present duties, and wire the Supervising Architect of the date of your leaving Denver, and also, in order that you may be communicated with if so desired, of the date of your arrival at Cheyenne, giving your address, and on the completion of your investigation submit full report, in writing, to the same officer.

Your actual traveling and subsistence expenses while in the performance of this service will be paid from an appropriation under the control of the Supervising Architect.

Respectfully,

H A Taylor

Assistant Secretary.

S.

T.

2 Lintels over Main Entrances	13'2" long x 2'10" x 2'0"
2 " " " "	9'6" " x 2'8" x 1'6"
2 " " " "	9'6" " x 1' 9" x 1'4-1/2"
6 Cornice Stones, 1st Story, Main Entr.	6'3" " x 5'10" x 2'8-1/2"
6 Monoliths Court Room Windows	13'6-3/4" x 1' 6" x 1'9"
20 " 3rd Story Windows	8'3-1/4" x 10" x 1'0"
20 " 2nd Story "	7'2" long x 1' 5" x 1'3"
8 Main Cornice Stones	7'7" " x 5' 0" x 1'9" 6?-?
4 " " " at corners	6'4" " x 6' 4" x 1'9" - ?? ?
10 Main Column Caps	3'8" " x 2'5" x 2'5"
4 Stones in Tablets	6'8" " x 2' 5" x 8"-?? ?
32 " " 1st Story Piers	7'10" " x 2'4" x 2'10-3/4"

Note.   The above dimensions are only approximate. For exact dimensions see drawings and F.S details.   May 18, 1901.

RECEIVED at CHEYENNE, WYO

⌐4.D.E.O 38 paid Govt

Washington D.C.May 24th,1901

Lee Ullery
            InterOcean Hotel,
                        Cheyenne,Wyo.

Not thought necessary to
visit Rawlins quarry.If Rawlins stone used in Cheyenne building
it satisfactory say so by wire from Cheyenne go to
Iron Mountain.

                James P.Low,
                        Acting Supervising Architect.

10:57A

DENVER NEW MINT.

*In replying to this Letter the
initials in upper right-hand
corner must be referred to.*

(ENCLOSURE 88)

The Superintendent of Construction,

    United States (new) Mint,

        Denver, Colorado.

Sir:

    I am in receipt of your letter of the 7th
ultimo, with enclosures from Mr. John A. McIntyre
relative to the method of fireproofing the steel
girders to be installed in the building under your
charge.

    In reply I have to state that the sketches
submitted do not show a proper method of fire-
proof construction, nor indicate the thickness
of the terra-cotta, and additional sketches must
therefore be submitted for approval in lieu of
those herewith returned.

    The shoe blocks should not be less than 1-1/2"
in thickness and must be clamped together at the
bottom of the girder.

        Respectfully,

                              Supervising Architect.

R.

Denver Colorade, June 5 1901

Lee Ullery Esq,

    Superintendent Construction.

        U. S. Mint (New) Denver Colo.

  Sir,

      In pursuance of your order dated May 31st. 1901, I
have this day removed John Roy, as foreman, of the work upon the
building under your direction, and substituted therefor Kloff
Saleen as Foreman.

  Trusting this change will meet your approval I am,

      very Respectfully.

Chas. A. Schieren.   F. A. M. Burrell.   Chas. A. Schieren

CHICAGO.
46-48 SO. CANAL ST
BOSTON.
119 HIGH ST.
PHILADELPHIA.
226 NORTH 3rd ST.
PITTSBURG, PA.
240 THIRD AVENUE.
BROOKLYN.
COR. 13 th ST. & 3 rd AVE.

OAK LEATHER TANNERIES.
BRISTOL, TENN.

Chas. A. Schieren & Co.

Tanners and Manufacturers of

Oak Leather Belting and Lace Leather.

45-51 Ferry Street & 7-8 Cliff Street.
1315-16th ST., DENVER, COLO.

~~New York,~~ June 3rd 1901

Mr. Lee Ullery,
Sup't of Construction,
U.S. Mint,
Denver, Colo.

Dear sir,

We beg to call your attention to our having opened a regular Branch, at 1315--16th ST., Denver, Colo., with a complete stock of Leather Belting and Lace Leather, of the highest grade, in each case. We should be glad to have you inspect the stock before buying the equipment of the new Mint.

We have supplied a great deal of belting to the various Departments of the Government. As an instance we may cite the equipment of the new Gun Factory at WASHINGTON, and the new Smokeless Powder Factory at Indian Head, Md. Our Belting has given perfect satisfaction wherever used in all the Navy Yards, and is up to the specifications in every particular.

All our Leather is tanned by the old, long process, with pure oak bark. This is conducive of the longest possible life in leather belting. With our facilities here we are able to take care of your every want in our line.

Hoping to hear from you, we are,

Yours respectfully,
CHAS. A. SCHIEREN & CO.
H. H. Geisse Mgr.

L.S. GILLETTE Mangr.
GEO M. GILLETTE, Ass't Mangr.

THE GILLETTE-HERZOG MANUFACTURING Co.

ENGINEERS AND BUILDERS OF STEEL
BRIDGES AND STRUCTURES.

STEEL SKELETON BUILDINGS, STEEL ROOFS STEEL AND COMBINATION BRIDGES
RIVETED TRUSSES AND PLATE GIRDERS, STEEL AND CAST IRON COLUMNS
MINING BUILDINGS, ORE CARS AND RIVETED PIPE
HEAVY AND LIGHT CASTINGS AND ALL KINDS OF FOUNDRY WORK.
STEEL BEAMS ANGLES PLATES BARS AND CORRUGATED IRON ALWAYS IN STOCK.
DESIGNS AND ESTIMATES FURNISHED ON APPLICATION.

OFFICE AND WORKS 2ND TO 9TH AVE S E
MINNEAPOLIS MINN.

18

Minneapolis, Minn. June 6, 1901.

Mr. Lee Ullery,

Supt. U. S. Mint,

Denver, Colo.

My Dear Sir:-

You are so accustomed to my troubling you by this time that you
won't mind once more. This time it is in reference to the iron gates which
were not within the Company's contract and which I left on the grounds last
March hoping the contractor of that part of the work to which the gates
belonged, would use them. What I wanted to ask you about is whether that
contract is about to be let and to whom, if you know, I might write in reference to taking the gates off the Company's hands.

Thanking you in advance, I am

Very sincerely yours,

THE GILLETTE-HERZOG MFG. CO.,

By

DENVER, COLO, MINT (new)

F

*In replying to this Letter the
initials in upper right-hand
corner must be referred to.*

TREASURY DEPARTMENT

OFFICE OF THE SUPERVISING ARCHITECT

Washington, June 7, 1901.

The Superintendent of Construction,
    U. S. Mint Building (new),
        Denver, Colorado.

Sir:

I have to direct that you will, on the last day of the present month, prepare and mail a letter addressed to this office giving briefly but explicitly the following information.

FIRST,   The point of advancement in each branch of the work at June 30th, 1901; and,

SECOND,   A brief synopsis of the work accomplished in the period between June 30th, 1900, (date of the last report) and June 30th, 1901.

It should be noted that quantities are not desired, but the statement should be prepared in such manner as will convey readily the condition of the work, for use in connection with the preparation of the annual report of operations on buildings under the control of this office under date of June 30th, 1901.

Should the advancement since date of last photograph be such as to warrant securing new views you are directed to submit an estimate of the cost of securing photographic views of the building in accordance with the spirit of Section VIII of printed "Instructions to Superintendents," in order that if so desired proper Departmental action may be taken authorizing you to incur a liability for obtaining views of the building, each negative to have scratched on the lower left hand corner, on the film side of the negative, the title and location of the building and the date, which must be June 30th, 1901.

Respectfully,

Supervising Architect.

Treasury Department,

OFFICE OF THE SUPERVISING ARCHITECT,

Washington, D. C., *June 7-1901*

Sir:

The receipt this day is hereby acknowledged of your communication of *June 3rd. Closet framer...*

and referring thereto you are informed that the matter will receive due consideration, and action will be taken at the earliest date.

Respectfully,

J. K. TAYLOR,
Supervising Architect.

Treasury Department,

OFFICE OF THE SUPERVISING ARCHITECT,

Washington, D. C., June 7, 1901,

Sir:

The receipt this day is hereby acknowledged of your communication of June 4, 1901, relative to wire for securing Spanish tile to roof of building under your charge,

and referring thereto you are informed that the matter will receive due consideration, and action will be taken at the earliest date.

Respectfully,

J. K. TAYLOR,
Supervising Architect.

Denver,Colo., June 12th,1901.

Lee Ullery,Esq.,

      Supt.Construction, United States Mint (New),

        Denver, Colorado.

Sir:-

      Referring to our conversation of some days ago,I have
the honor to say that I will make five (5) tie rods for stair plat-
form between 2nd and 3rd floors,in the U.S.Mint building now under
construction,and put same in place complete,to receive the Terra
Cotta Floor Arches,for the sum of ten dollars ($10.00).

               Very Respectfully,

               (Signed) J.A.McIntyre

                      T.

DENVER. P.O. & CT.H.

B

*In replying to this Letter the
initials in upper right-hand
corner must be referred to.*

TREASURY DEPARTMENT

OFFICE OF THE SUPERVISING ARCHITECT

Washington,   June 7, 1901.

22

Superintendent of Construction,

U. S. Mint (new),

Denver, Colorado.

Sir:

Your report of the 3rd instant is received, relating to the proposed construction of closets under stairs in the Post Office and Court House building in your city, and in accordance with your recommendations the proposals for this work, transmitted in the Custodian's letter of the 24th ultimo, have been rejected.

You are now directed to prepare a specification for constructing these closets, following the lines of your report, and to hand the same to the Custodian, who has been authorized upon its receipt to take new proposals for the performance of the work.

Respectfully,

Supervising Architect.

AUTHORITY FOR OPEN-MARKET PURCHASE.

(All letters in reply to official communications must refer to initial in upper right-hand corner.)

Treasury Department,

OFFICE OF THE SUPERVISING ARCHITECT,

Washington, D. C., **June 14, 1901.**

The Superintendent of Construction,

U.S. Mint Building, (new),

Denver,Colorado.

Sir:

In view of the request and recommendation contained in your letter of the 8th instant,and the public exigency requiring the immediate delivery of the articles and performance of the work you are hereby authorized to incur an expenditure of five dollars ($5.00)

in securing in open market at lowest prevailing rates:

photographic views of work on the building, $ 5.00

Your attention is called to printed "Instructions to Superintendents," and you will issue and certify vouchers on account of the above in accordance therewith,payment to be made from the appropriation for " Mint Building,Denver, Colo."

Respectfully yours

Acting Chief Executive Officer.

JOHN A. MCINTYRE,
GENERAL CONTRACTOR.
OMS 402-404 COOPER BUILDING.
DENVER, COLO.
Telephone 1238.

OWNER AND OPERATOR
ARKINS GRANITE QUARRIES.

Copy

Denver Colorado, June 14 1901.

Hon. J. K. Taylor,

    Supervising Architect,

        Washington, D. C.

       Sir,

      After a careful examination of the plans and specification for the foundation, superstructure and roof covering of the U. S. Mint (New) this city, under my contract with the United States I have the honor to request that I be permitted to omit from said contract the following.

Granite steps in basement, The tearing down and rebuilding of the defective portion of Chimney "C", the stone for which are to be fully cut and stored according to the directions of the superintendent of Construction, and the omission of the 8" T. C. partition from column 18 to South wall.

In consideration of which permission for omission I agree to deduct from the sum total of my original contract the sum of One Hundred and Seventy-five ($175.00) Dollars.

Without predjudice of any of the rights of the United States.

          Very respectfully,

           J. A. McIntyre.

DENVER, COLO., NEW MINT.

TREASURY DEPARTMENT

OFFICE OF THE SUPERVISING ARCHITECT

Washington, June 12, 1901.

Superintendent of Construction,
     New Mint,
          Denver, Colorado.

Sir:

Referring to your letter of the 4th instant, and to the
samples of wire forwarded therewith, which, as you state con-
forms with the requirements of the specification provided the
Browne and Sharpe gauge is considered as standard, you are
advised that in the absence of any other requirement the Browne
& Sharpe or American standard will govern, therefore, your
action in allowing the use of the material in question, is
approved.

Respectfully,

Supervising Architect.

Form No. 175.
Ed. 3 22 1901 5,000.

Treasury Department,

OFFICE OF THE SUPERVISING ARCHITECT.

Washington, D. C., June 13, 1901.

Sir:

The receipt this day is hereby acknowledged of your communication of the 8th instant, relative to data for annual report and securing photographic views of work on the building under your charge, and referring thereto you are informed that the matter will receive due consideration, and action will be taken at the earliest date.

Respectfully,

J. K. TAYLOR,
Supervising Architect.

DENVER,COLO.,NEW MINT.

ENCLOSURE 1962.

TREASURY DEPARTMENT

OFFICE OF THE SUPERVISING ARCHITECT

Washington,   June 17, 1901.

Superintendent of Construction,
     New Mint Building,
          Denver, Colorado.

Sir:

     This Office is in receipt of a letter of the 14th instant,
from Mr. John A. McIntyre, contractor for the foundations, superstructure and roof covering of the building in your charge,
a copy of which is enclosed herewith and explains itself, and
you are requested to forward to this Office your recommendation relative to the matter referred to therein.

                         Respectfully,

                              Supervising Architect.

M.T.R.

O P Y .

EADING.

Denver, Colorado, June 14,1901.

Hon.J.K.Taylor,
    Supervising Architect,
        Washington, D.C.

Sir:

After a careful examination of the plans and specifications for the Foundations,Superstructure and Roof Covering of
the U.S.Mint (New) this city, under my contract with the
United States I have the honor to request that I be permitted
to omit from said contract, the following.

Granite steps in basement,The tearing down and rebuilding of
the defective portion of Chimney "C", the stone for which are
to be fully cut and stored according to the directions of the
Superintendent of Construction, and the omission of the 8"
T.C. partition from Column 18 to South wall.

In consideration of which permission for omission I agree to
deduct from the sum total of my original contract the sum of
One Hundred and Seventy five ($175.00) Dollars.

Without prejudice to any of the rights of the United States.

                        Very respectfully,

                            (Signed) J.A.McIntyre.

                                T.

Copied by M.T.R.

Denver, Colorado, June 14,1901.

Hon.J.K.Taylor,
    Supervising Architect,
        Washington, D.C.

Sir:

After a careful examination of the plans and specifications for the Foundations,Superstructure and Roof Covering of
the U.S.Mint (New) this city, under my contract with the
United States I have the honor to request that I be permitted
to omit from said contract, the following.

Granite steps in basement,The tearing down and rebuilding of
the defective portion of Chimney "C", the stone for which are
to be fully cut and stored according to the directions of the
Superintendent of Construction, and the omission of the 8"
T.C. partition from Column 18 to South wall.

In consideration of which permission for omission I agree to
deduct from the sum total of my original contract the sum of
One Hundred and Seventy five ($175.00) Dollars.

Without prejudice to any of the rights of the United States.

Very respectfully,

(Signed) J.A.McIntyre.

T.

Copied by M.T.R.

PRINTED HEADING.

Denve, Colorado, June 21st,1901.

Hon.J.K.Taylor,

     Supervising Architect, Washington, D.C.

Sir:-

In order to rectify my inadvertence,in forwarding proposition
of the 14th inst. direct to you instead of through the office of the
Superintendent of Construction,and as substitute for any and all previous propositions on the same subject, I have the honor to request
that I be allowed to omit from my contract the following.

Ist.   The 8 inch terra cotta partition in basement from col.18 to
      south wall.

2nd.   The remaining work on chimney "C".provided, that the defec-
      tive portion be taken down,and all granite therefor be cut
      and stored on the building site.

3rd.   Three granite steps in basement.

In consideration of permission for such omission, I agree to
deduct from the total contract price allowed me the sum of One Hundred
and seventy five ($175) dollars,without prejudice to any of the rights
of the United States.

               Very respectfully,

               (Signed) J.A.McIntyre,
                        T.

DENVER MINT (new)

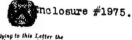
TREASURY DEPARTMENT,

OFFICE OF THE SUPERVISING ARCHITECT,

Washington,   June 19, 1901.

Superintendent of Construction,
         New Mint Building,
             Denver, Colorado.

Sir:-

I enclose herewith, for your information and the files of
your office, a copy of Department letter of even date, accepting
the proposal of John A. McIntyre, the contractor for the foundation, superstructure and roof covering of the building in your
charge, in amount ten dollars ($10.00), to place five tie rods
for stair platforms between the second and third floors to receive the terra cotta arches, all as stated in the said letter
of acceptance.

You are hereby authorized to certify and issue vouchers
on account of the work, as required by the terms of the contract
and the printed "Instructions to Superintendents," payment of
which vouchers the Disbursing Agent has been authorized to
make from the appropriation for Mint Building, Denver, Colo.

Respectfully,

Supervising Architect.

J.S.S.

June 19,1901.

Mr. John A.McIntyre,
    Cooper Building,
        Denver,Colorado.

Sir:-

In view of the statement and recommendation contained in letter of the 18th instant from the Superintendent of Construction of the new Mint Building at Denver,Colorado, your proposal, of the same date, addressed to him, in amount ten dollars (say), is hereby accepted to place five (5) his rods for stair platforms between the second and third floors to receive the terra cotta arches, the same being deemed reasonable and a public exigency requiring an immediate performance of the work, which is to be considered an addition to your contract dated March 29,1898 for the foundation, superstructure and roof covering of the said building.

It is understood and agreed that this addition is not to affect the time for the completion of the work as required by the terms of your contract, that the same is without prejudice to any and all rights of the United States thereunder; and without prejudice,also, to any and all rights of the United States against the sureties on the bond executed for the faithful fulfillment of the contract.

Please promptly acknowledge the receipt of this letter.
                                        Respectfully,

J.C.P.
                                        Secretary..

TREASURY DEPARTMENT,

OFFICE OF THE SUPERVISING ARCHITECT

*In replying to this Letter the
initials in upper right-hand
corner must be referred to.*

Washington,   June 19, 1901.

Inclosure 580.

Mr. Lee Ullery,

    Superintendent of Construction,

        Mint Building, Denver, Colorado.

Sir:-

    I enclose herewith Disbursing Clerk George A. Bartlett's check, No. 188068, dated June 18, 1901, drawn to your order, in the sum of...$25.40, for expenses incurred by you in traveling from Denver, Colorado, to Cheyenne, Wyoming, and return, under orders from this Department.

    Please acknowledge receipt.

                Respectfully,

                    Acting Chief Executive Officer.

F.D.

(All letters in reply to official communications must refer to initial in upper right-hand corner.)

Treasury Department,   F

Office of the Supervising Architect,

Washington, D. C.,   June 22, 1901.

The Superintendent of Construction,

    Mint Building, (new),

        Denver, Colorado.

Sir:

    Please fill up the enclosed blank, and return immediately to this office, giving the information as relates to members of the contingent force named below under your charge, the information being desired in the preparation of the "Official Register of the United States.

                                JAS. A. WETMORE.

                            Acting Chief Executive Officer.

Lee Ullery,	Superintendent.
Oscar Hinrichs,	Clerk,
Herbert E. Quigley,	Inspector,
Eugene C. Wilson,	Watchman,
Benjamin Tuthill,	do
James L. Hodges,	Disbursing Agent.

...THE...
COLORADO PORTLAND CEMENT COMPANY.
Works at Portland, Colorado.

TRADE MARK

Denver, Colo., June 27_____1901_

Mr. Lee Ullery,

    Supt. Denver Mint, Denver, Colo.

    Dear Sir:-

        Some time ago at your suggestion we wrote to Mr. Roberts at San Francisco asking him to make tests on our cement. We now have his reply which is as follows:

        "Referring to your letter of the 15th instant, you are advised that I have made a seven day test (24 hours in air and 6 days in water) of six briquettes from the sample of cement forwarded by you under that date, with the following results as to tensile strength:-

670 lbs.	700 lbs.	750 lbs.
700 "	725 "	820 "

28 day test:-

870 lbs.	880 lbs.	900 lbs."

        Thinking you may be interested in these tests we send them to you as you will see the tests prove very satisfactory. Thanking you for your interest in this matter we remain,

                Yours truly,

form 32.
Ed. 13-20-'94—2,000.}

34

Treasury Department,

OFFICE OF THE SUPERVISING ARCHITECT,

Washington, D. C.,   June 25, 1901.

Mr. Lee Ullery,

Supt. U. S. Mint Building,

Denver, Colorado.

Sir:

I have to acknowledge the receipt of your "Estimate of Funds" required for the work on the building under your superintendence during the month of June, 1901, ~~19XX~~, *and to advise you that, as it appears the remittance of funds heretofore made to the Disbursing Agent on account of the appropriation for the building is sufficient to meet all vouchers issued or to be issued for expenditures on account of the work on the building, to and including the last day of the current month, no further remittance will be made to him at present.*

B.

Respectfully, yours,

Jas. A. Turlenton

Acting *Chief Executive Officer.*

F.D.

Form No. 177.
Ed. 3-22-1901 1,000.

Treasury Department,

OFFICE OF THE SUPERVISING ARCHITECT,

Washington, D. C., *June 25-01.*

Sir:

The receipt this day is hereby acknowledged of your communication of *the 21 inst submitting proposals to omit three granite steps in basement eight terra cotta partitions &c,*

and referring thereto you are informed that the matter will receive due consideration, and action will be taken at the earliest date.

Respectfully,

J. P. Low

Acting Supervising Architect.

Form No. 175.
Ed. 3-22-1901 6,000.

Treasury Department,

OFFICE OF THE SUPERVISING ARCHITECT,

Washington, D. C., June 24, 1901.

Sir:

The receipt this day is hereby acknowledged of your communication of the 20th instant, relative terra cotta at openings, etc.,

and referring thereto you are informed that the matter will receive due consideration, and action will be taken at the earliest date.

Respectfully,

J. K. TAYLOR,
Supervising Architect.

Form No. 175.
Ed. 3-22-1901 6,000.

Treasury Department,

OFFICE OF THE SUPERVISING ARCHITECT,

Washington, D. C., June 24, 1901.

Sir:

The receipt this day is hereby acknowledged of your communication of the 21st instant, relative proposals for granite steps, &c

and referring thereto you are informed that the matter will receive due consideration, and action will be taken at the earliest date.

Respectfully,

DENVER (new) Mint.

TREASURY DEPARTMENT

OFFICE OF THE SUPERVISING ARCHITECT

Washington,   June 27,1901.

The Superintendent of Construction,

    United States (new) Mint,

       Denver, Colorado.

Sir:

    I am in receipt of your letter of the 20th instant relative to the construction of certain terra-cotta openings in the first floor of the building under your charge,and the action taken in the matter is hereby approved.

    The statement regarding the iron work for the first and second floors has been noted,and a clause will be inserted in the specification for painting the tops of beams referred to.

        Respectfully,

        Acting Supervising Architect.

R.

Treasury Department.

Mr. Lee Ullery

    Superintendent, Construction, U.S. Public Buildings,

        c/o Supervising Architect.

Sir:

    Section 5 of the Act of Congress, approved March 2, 1895,
"making appropriations for the legislative, executive, and judi-
cial expenses of the Government for the fiscal year ending June
30, 1896, and for other purposes," provides that "hereafter every
officer whose duty it is to take and approve official bonds shall
cause all such bonds to be renewed every four years after their
dates, but he may require such bonds to be renewed or strength-
ened oftener if he deem such action necessary."

    Your current bond as   Superintendent of Construction, United
States Public Buildings

will have run for a period of four years on   July 2, 1901. You
are accordingly hereby directed to execute a new bond as such,
with good and sufficient surety in the penal sum of   five
thousand dollars, and forward the same to this office as early as
practicable in order that any necessary alterations or correc-
tions may be made to perfect it for formal approval and acceptance on July 3, 1901.

       Respectfully, yours,

                        Acting Secretary

T.

DENVER, NEW MINT.

ENCLOSURE 2426.

TREASURY DEPARTMENT

OFFICE OF THE SUPERVISING ARCHITECT

Washington,   July 1, 1901.

Superintendent of Construction,
   New Mint Building,
      Denver, Colorado.

Sir:

    I enclose herewith, for your information and the files of
your office, a copy of Department letter of the 29th ultimo, accepting the proposal of Mr. John A. McIntyre to deduct the sum of
one hundred and seventy-five dollars ($175.00) from the amount
to be paid him under his contract for the foundation, superstructure and roof covering of the building in your charge, on
account of certain omissions as stated in detail in said letter of acceptance, which explains itself.

        Respectfully,

        Acting Supervising Architect.

M.T.R.

June 29, 1901.

Mr. John A. McIntyre,
   Cooper Building,
     Denver, Colorado.

Sir:-

In view of the statement and recommendation contained in letter of June 21,1901 from the Superintendent of Construction of the new Mint Building at Denver, Colorado, and in accordance with the approval of this Department, your proposal, of the same date, addressed to the Supervising Architect, is hereby accepted to deduct the sum of one hundred and seventy-five dollars ($175.00) from the amount to be paid you under your contract dated March 29, 1899 for the foundation, superstructure and roof covering of the said building, on account of the following named omissions, the same being deemed reasonable and a public exigency requiring the changes, namely:

Omit the 8" terra cotta partition in basement from column 11 in south wall;
Omit the remaining work on chimney "C," provided that defective portion be taken down, and all granite therefor be out and stored on the building site;
Omit three granite steps in basement.

It is understood and agreed that this deduction is not to affect the time for the completion of the work as required by the terms of your contract; that the same is without prejudice to any and all rights of the United States thereunder; and without prejudice, also, to any and all rights of the United States against the sureties on the bond executed for the faithful fulfillment of the

John A. McIntyre, Page 2.

Please promptly acknowledge the receipt of this letter, a copy of which will be forwarded to the Superintendent, for his information and guidance.

Respectfully,

R.
J.N.P.   Acting Secretary.

J.F.S.

THE WESTERN UNION TELEGRAPH COMPANY.

RECEIVED at 1114 to 1118 17th St., Denver, Colo.   **NEVER CLOSED.**

46-A.   MH.   GT.   34 Paid govt   642

Washington,D .C, Jan 25-1901.

Supt Ullery,

New Mint, Denver, Colo.

Ulm stand stone Quarry Cascade county Montana at Ponca
Telegraph capacity of quarry, quality of stone. drawings at Assayer's
ce Helena answer.

H.A.Taylor,Ass't sec'y.

12 p.m.

TELEGRAM

19j b v, 36 collect 44, 5ex Govt

Washington, D.C. June 26/01-27. Via Denver, Colo

Supt Ullery,
U. S. Assay office, Helena, Mont.

After telegraphing report on Ulm visit Montana Sand Stone quarry
Columbus, Montana, and report by wire, answer.

H. A. Taylor,
Asst Secy.
3:05 pm

Denver Colorado. July 8 1901.

Lee Ullery Supt. Const.

    Denver Mint (new) Denver,

        Colorado.

Sir,

    Replying to your letter 5th. inst. I have the honor to say,
that as I understand the matter, the omission of the several
stones, was permitted under an agreement with Mr. Baines, the
Granite Fore-man. As I understand however, that conditions have
changed, I desire that the matter may be held in suspense,
without further action, pending the arrival of the incoming
contractor, for the completion of the building, when he can be
consulted and arrangements made with him if necessary.

              Very Respectfully,

In replying to this Letter the
initials in upper right-hand
corner must be referred to.

TREASURY DEPARTMENT

OFFICE OF THE SUPERVISING ARCHITECT

Washington,   July 8, 1901.

Superintendent of Construction,

    United States Mint,

        Denver, Colo.

Sir:-

    You are advised that the Custodian of the Post Office and
Court House in your city, has been authorized to accept the proposal
of John J. Bitter, in amount $195.00, for constructing closets under
the stairs in that building, in accordance with specification prepared by you, and you are requested to aid the Custodian in the
supervision of the work, checking the vouchers, therefor, upon satisfactory completion.

                Respectfully,

                     Acting Supervising Architect.

The Mint Department

... The Secretary

Washington, July 3,1901.

Superintendent of Construction,

U.S.Mint (New),

Denver, Colorado.

Sir:

When your duties will permit and on or about the 12th instant, you are directed to visit the Land-Office, at Pueblo, Colorado, and Mr H.Mitchell, Custodian, where you will make an examination of work and material supplied under an agreement with Joseph Bochenager, for grilles and gratings and wire screen enclosure. Full information in regard to which will be found on the Custodian's files.

Please submit a report of the result of your visit, for the information and guidance of the Department in giving consideration to final settlement, and if entire and satisfactory completion of the work has been secured by the date of your visit, request the Custodian to forward the voucher in settlement.

Upon completion of this duty return to Denver, Colorado.

Your actual traveling and subsistance expenses while in the performance of this duty will be paid from appropriations under the charge of the Supervising Architect of this Department.

Respectfully,

DENVER. MINT (NEW).

B

In replying to this Letter the
initials in upper right-hand
corner must be referred to.

TREASURY DEPARTMENT

OFFICE OF THE SUPERVISING ARCHITECT

Washington, July 10, 1901.

Superintendent of Construction,

    U. S. Mint (new),

        Denver, Colorado.

Sir:

      During the interval since date of receipt of your letter
of April 20th last in relation to terra cotta for floor arches to
be supplied for the building under your charge, as embraced in a
contract with John A. McIntyre, an analysis of the sample submitted
by you has been made with the result that it is necessary that you
exercise extreme care in the acceptance or rejection of the material
referred to.   Such care by you is evidently contemplated by the
concluding paragraph of your letter referred to, and you are now
requested to make a thorough and satisfactory test of arches throughout the building and to permit none to remain where the integrity of
the same is at all in question.

              Respectfully,

              Acting Supervising Architect.

Office of Custodian

U. S. Court-House and Post-Office.

PUEBLO, COLO.

JUL 15 1901 ———, 189

Lee Ullery Esq
            Supt. U. S. Mint,
                    Denver, Colo,
Dear Sir,

            In reply to yours of
14" relative to procuring com-
-petition in the proposals
for repairs to area walls
and railings, will say that
Mr. Summers and Mr.
Hochnauer will bid on
same and I hope to forward
the proposals by Tomorrow,
            Respy
            F. A. Townsend
            Acting Custodian

DENVER. NEW MINT.

MGD

In replying to this Letter the
initials in upper right-hand
corner must be referred to.

TREASURY DEPARTMENT

OFFICE OF THE SUPERVISING ARCHITECT

Washington, July 12, 1901.

The Superintendent of Construction,

U. S. Mint (New),

Denver, Col.

Sir:

You are requested to forward to this office, at as early a
date as practicable, a sample of surface well water taken from a
well or from wells in immediate proximity to the building under
your charge; and, in addition thereto, a sample of artesian well
water from the same vicinity, if procurable.   Samples should be
not less than one gallon each.

Respectfully,

Acting Supervising Architect.

DIVISION OF STATIONERY, PRINTING, AND BLANKS. }
Form No. 103.—Ed. 9 15 1900 1,000. }

NOTIFICATION THAT ENVELOPES HAVE BEEN ORDERED FROM CONTRACTORS.

Treasury Department,
OFFICE OF THE SECRETARY.

Washington,_____July 12 , 190 1

Sir:

The envelopes specified in your requisition of _____July 12_____, 190 1
have this day been ordered from the contractors, to be delivered to you direct,
upon a Government bill of lading. When received, a sample of each size and
kind must be forwarded immediately, with the receipted stationery invoice,
to the Department for examination. See Department Circular No. 104 of
1899.

Respectfully,

Chief of Division of Stationery, Printing, and Blanks.

Per

Form No. 177. }
Ed. 2 23 1901 4,000. }

Sir:

The receipt _____

nication of July _____

and referring _____

receive due _____

JOHN A. MCINTYRE,
GENERAL CONTRACTOR,
ROOMS 402-404 COOPER BUILDING,
DENVER, COLO.
Telephone 1238.
OWNER AND OPERATOR
AKKINS GRANITE QUARRIES.

Denver Colo, July 17 1901.

Lee Ullery Esq.

    Supt. Con. New Mint.

        Denver Colo.

Sir,

    I have the honor to acknowledge receipt of your le
16th inst. regarding grades at U. S. Mint Building.

    I will give the matter careful attention, and communicate
you regarding same, within the next few days.

        very Respectfully.

PRINTED HEADING.

Denver,Colo., July 16,1901.

Lee Ullery,Esq.,
Superintendent of Construction,
U.S.Mint (New), Denver, Colo.

Sir:-

Replying to your letter May 13th,ultimo,calling my attention to "defective condition of concrete and cement covering of coal
vault" U.S.Mint building,this city,and requiring me to remedy same,
I have the honor to say.

I have carefully investigated the matter,and from the facts
presented to my notice,and led to believe that said alleged defective
condition,is in no way my fault,nor under the terms of my contract,
should I be held responsible therefor.

The specifications under which the work is progressing
provide on page seven (7) as follows:

"Area floors to have 8" thick layer of concrete graded to the out-
lets with 1" thick coat of equal parts coarse sand and Portland cement trowled smooth and jointed to the cesspools.

The top of the coal vault to be leveled up with concrete,and finished with a 2" thick coat of mortar as specified for the area floors.

"The concrete is to be mixed in batches,quickly laid in place,and
thoroughly tamped into a compact mass until free mortar appears on
the surface".

These provisions appear to be the only ones in the specification applying to this portion of the work.
THE CONTRACT for the foundation,superstructure and roof-covering of
the U.S.Mint building,this city,of which the specifications referred
to are a part, provides on lines 1,2,&,3, as follows:

that the work performed shall be executed in the most skillful and workmanlike manner; and that both the materials used and the work performed shall be to the entire and complete satisfaction of the said Supervising Architect".

Said CONTRACT,further provides,lines 45 to 48,both inclusive,as follows:

"It is further covenanted and agreed by and between the parties hereto, that the materials furnished and the work done under this contract shall be subject to the inspection of the Supervising Architect,the Superintendent of the building and other inspectors, by appointed the said party of the first part,with the right to reject any and all work or materials not in accordance with this contract; AND THE SAID DECISION OF SAID SUPERVISING ARCHITECT AS TO QUALITY AND QUANTITY SHALL BE FINAL".

Said contract further provides lines 48 to 55 inclusive,that the party of the second part shall at his own expense and within a reasonable time remove or remedy defective or unsatisfactory work, and provides a penalty for his refusal to do so.
In order therefore,that the penalty so provided may not attach in this case,and that I may be construed to have taken action within the reasonable time, referred to, I make you the following statement.
I am informed and believe,and therefore state the fact to be,that the work complained of in your said letter of May 13th, was performed during your absence,under the personal supervision of your representative and that of the Supervising Architect, Mr.Herbert E.Quigley,Granite Inspector.
That said concrete was skillfully prepared in a workmanlike manner "in batches",from approved materials,in proper proportions,as called for by the specifications,and quickly laid in place and thoroughly tamped into a compact mass,until free mortar appeared on the surface.
That each batch of said concrete was prepared and laid under the eye of and was personally inspected by Inspector Quigley,and was approved by him.
I am further informed and believe the fact to be,that prior to the laying of the 2" thick coat of mortar called for in said specifications that said Quigley was advised by the sub-foreman in charge of the work, (who had been specially selected on account of his great skill and good workmanship) that owing to the fact that said 2" coating was bound -ed on all sides by immovable granite walls,allowing of absolutely no expansion,that cracks and raises or "bubbles" would surely result if said Inspector required the laying of said coat in "one continuous body". That the proper and workmanlike manner of laying said coat was in alternate panels of convenient size,allowing same to expand and contract in setting,and after the said setting had progressed to a given

point,the laying in a similar manner of the alternate panels previous
-ly omitted.
That this manner of workmanship would insure a tight,well finished
job,free of cracks and defects,while the method indicated by said
Quigley would result in the very defects sought to be avoided.
I further allege the facts to be, that said Quigley admitted,that
the method of panelling "MIGHT" be the better plan,but declared that
he was powerless to deviate from the specifications which called for
a continuous body,and that the work must therefore be done as indicated by him. That thereupon, by my personal order,the sub-foreman
in charge of said work, notified said Quigley,in the presence of wit-
nesses,that he would perform the work as indicated,but that he (Quigley) must assume responsibility for any and all defects resulting
from the method of work required.
That said work was performed as indicated by said Inspector,and under
his personal,continuous and careful inspection,and was from time to
time approved and accepted by him as the work progressed.
Such then,being the facts,it seems
1st. that,there being nothing in the specifications distinctly re-
         quiring the laying of said 2" thick coat in a continuous body,
that said Quigley exceeded his authority in demanding that said work
be performed in the manner indicated,especially in the face of a
specific protest from skilled workmen in charge of the work.
2nd. That said Quigley as the representative of the Supervising Archi-
         tect, having in the face of a formal protest,demanded the per-
formance of the work in a manner not called for by the specifications
and having inspected and approved said work,during construction,"said
decision of the Supervising Architect as to quality and quantity shall
be FINAL and I am by his action relieved from further responsibility
therefor.
3rd. That said Quigley exceeded his authority in dictating to workmen
the manner in which they should perform their labors,and such action
was on a par with the method of inspection pursued by him at the Granite Yards,where his interference with the men and their work has caused great loss to me as a contractor,and has been the subject of com-
plaint made to you in my behalf by my representative Mr.Scott Truxtun.
I have therefore the honor to protest against the requirement of your
said letter of May 13th,ultimo, and to appeal from your said decision
to the Hon.Supervising Architect for final adjustment.

                        Very respectfully,
                        (Signed)John A.McIntyre
                        By G.E.Ross-Lewin,Atty.

Form 34.
M. & N W & No. }

ADVISING OF REMITTANCE OF FUNDS.
— ——————————— --

J.

Treasury Department,

OFFICE OF SUPERVISING ARCHITECT,

Washington, D. C.,   July 19, 1901., 1900xx

Sir:

Your estimate of funds required during the month of   July, 1901,

190xx, *for the work under your charge, is received. I have to advise you that a*

remittance of $ 20,000   TTT *to*   Mr. James L. Hodges,

Disbursing Agent, has been requested.

Respectfully yours,

Jas. A. Wetmore
Acting *Chief Executive Officer.*

Mr. Lee Ullery,

Superintendent *U. S.* Mint Building,
Denver, Colorado.

F.D.

TREASURY DEPARTMENT
OFFICE OF THE SECRETARY

Washington,   July 19, 1901.

Mr. Lee Ullery,

    C/o Supervising Architect,

        Treasury Department.

Sir:-

    By direction of the Secretary, I have to inform you that
your official bond as Superintendent of Construction, United
States Public Buildings, given in the penal sum of five thous-
and dollars ($5,000), and bearing date of July 3, 1901, was
approved by the Secretary July 18, 1901.

        Respectfully,

                Chief, Division of Appointments.

TREASURY DEPARTMENT

OFFICE OF THE SUPERVISING ARCHITECT

In replying to this Letter the
initials in upper right-hand
corner must be referred to.

Washington,   July 20, 1901.

Enclosure 760.

Mr. Lee Ullery,

  Superintendent of Construction,

    Mint Building, Denver, Colorado.

Sir:-

   I enclose herewith Disbursing Clerk George A.
Bartlett's check, No. 189226, dated July 19, 1901, drawn to
your order, in the sum of.........................$113.35,
for expenses incurred by you in traveling under orders from
this Department.

   Please acknowledge receipt.

     Respectfully,

          Acting Chief Executive Officer.

F.D.

Denver, Colo., July 23rd, 1901.

Lee Ullery, Esq.,
     United States Mint (New),
          Denver, Colorado.

Dear Sir:-
          Referring to our conversation of a day or two ago, regarding
the condition of stone "P.14-E", found cracked in the building, I have
the honor to say:
          Said stone was carefully inspected during its cutting and laying
and the imperfection causing the break if it existed then (as in my
opinion it did) was of such a nature as to be invisible to the naked
eye, and therefore beyond detection by ordinary intelligence.
          Had the crack been caused by insufficient or uneven bedding, and
the consequent concentration of the strain from the superstructure,
the break would, in my opinion, have appeared at some other point, not,
as it has done, nearly mid-way between joints and in the center of the
longest bed where breakage from strain appears to be impossible.
          In my opinion the break has been caused by a powder shake in
quarrying and may or may not go entirely through the stone. I have
the honor to suggest that the stone having been in place for at least
one year past, has thoroughly settled, all the brick backing has become a homogeneous mass and no further cracking or settling is possible.
          To attempt to remove this backing, cut loose the various cramps
and anchors, drill out the stone and replace it with another, with
fresh mortar and brick backing, would in my opinion be a very danger-
ous operation, entailing the possibility of further and extensive
cracks in the building.
          I have the honor to submit for your inspection a photograph of
a portion of the building showing the stone in question, which said
photograph I believe shows the crack fairly and in due proportion to
the size of the various joints surrounding the same. I believe that
by using a specially prepared Portland cement, properly mixed with
powdered granite to insure uniformity and match of color, carefully
filling the crack therewith and afterwards redressing the face of the
stone, that the defect can be rendered invisible to the eye and as im-
pervious to moisture as the native stone, and that the general safety
of the building can be more thoroughly insured than if it is attempted
to replace the stone in question by new and green material, with the
insufficient beds sure to be obtained from this class of work.
          I have the honor to ask then that I be allowed to try the plan
suggested herein, when, if the result proves unsatisfactory, I shall
of course be ready to adopt such other methods as may be considered
advisable.
          Trusting you may find it consistent to recommend to the Depart-
ment the course of action indicated, I am
                    Very respectfully,
                         (Signed) J.A.McIntyre,
                         Per G.E.Ross-Lewin, Att'y.

PUEBLO,COLO.,P.O.

Enclosure 773.

TREASURY DEPARTMENT

OFFICE OF THE SUPERVISING ARCHITECT

Washington,   July 23, 1901.

Mr. Lee Ullery,

      Superintendent of Construction,

         Mint Building,

           Denver, Colorado.

Sir:-

      I enclose herewith Disbursing Clerk Thomas J.
Hobbs' check, No. 198064, dated July 22, 1901, drawn to your
order, in the sum of...............................$14.65,
for expenses incurred by you in traveling from Denver to
Pueblo, Colorado, and return, under orders from this Department.

      Please acknowledge receipt.

           Respectfully,

                Acting Chief Executive Officer.

TREASURY DEPARTMENT

OFFICE OF THE SUPERVISING ARCHITECT

Washington,

July 26, 1901.

Superintendent of Construction,

    U. S. Mint (New),

        Denver, Colo.

Sir:

    Your communication of the 20th instant is received inclosing
copy of a letter addressed by you on May 13th, last, to Mr. J. A.
McIntyre, contractor for the foundation, superstructure and roof
covering of the building under your charge, demanding from him the
remedying of defective cement work over the coal vault, and his
reply thereto, dated the 16th instant, declining to comply with your
demand.

    The action taken by you in the matter is approved, and it is
requested that you will repeat your demand upon the contractor, and
inform him that in the event of his failure to remedy this defective
work, it will not be accepted and payment for the same will not be
made.

    The contract entered into by Mr. McIntyre requires that all
materials and workmanship must be first class and to the satisfaction
of the Supervising Architect. In this case the workmanship is not
first class and not to my satisfaction.

        Respectfully,

JOHN A. McINTYRE,
GENERAL CONTRACTOR,
ROOMS 402-404 COOPER BUILDING.
DENVER, COLO.
Telephone 1238.
OWNER AND OPERATOR
ARKINS GRANITE QUARRIES.

Denver Colorado, July 30 1901.

Lee Ullery Esq.

    Superintendent Construction

        United States Mint (New)

    Denver----------------Colorado.

        Sir.

            Replying to your letter July 29th. inst. advising
me that you are instructed by the Supervising Architect to
demand the remedying of certain defective work in cement covering
over coal vault, and to refuse payment for same, unless such
action is had; I have the honor to say.

I shall proceed to perform the work indicated UNDER PROTEST,
with the intention of applying to the Department for extra compen
sation therefor, on the ground of unjustifiable interference with
the work by the government representative, and, such being the
case, I respectfully request that you officially advise me in
writing of just what you desire in the matter, in order that
there may be no misunderstanding, and that I can at once proceed
with the work called for.

            Very Respectfully,

            John A. McIntyre
            Per W. E. Cary.

TREASURY DEPARTMENT,

OFFICE OF THE SUPERVISING ARCHITECT,

Washington, **August 6, 1901.**

The Superintendent of Construction,

United States Mint,

Denver, Colorado.

Sir:

In reply to your communication of August 2nd, 1901, referring to doorways in terra-cotta partitions, under the contract of J.A. McIntyre for the building under your charge, I have to advise you that the height of door openings Nos. 7 and 8, as well as Nos. 6 and 9, will be determined by the 12" channels connecting columns Nos. 10 and 15, and columns Nos. 33 and 38; this will give sufficient height for these doors and the interior details will be arranged to correspond.

In regard to opening No. 11, I have to say that as this opening will be closed up under the interior finish contract, the passage into which it opens having been done away with, there will be no necessity for making any change in its dimensions.

Respectfully,

Supervising Architect.

F.

DENVER,COLO.,NEW MINT.

In replying to this Letter the
initials in upper right-hand
corner must be referred to.

TREASURY DEPARTMENT

OFFICE OF THE SUPERVISING ARCHITECT

Washington, August 6, 1901.

Superintendent of Construction,

New Mint Building,
Denver, Colorado.

Sir:

I have to acknowledge the receipt of your letter of the
2nd instant, relative to including in a future specification
certain raglets which it hasbeen necessary to omit from the
contract of Mr. J.A.McIntyre for foundations, superstructure,
and roof covering at the building in your charge.

In reply you are advised that what you say has been noted
and the matter will be considered in placing work on the market
in the future.

Respectfully,

Supervising Architect.

M.T.R.

TREASURY DEPARTMENT,

OFFICE OF THE SUPERVISING ARCHITECT,

Washington,   August 14, 1901.

The Superintendent of Construction,

United States Mint,

Denver, Colorado.

Sir:

I have to acknowledge your communication of the
9th instant in regard to height of doorways Nos. 8 and 9,
for the building under your charge, and have to say that
this matter will be taken up at a later date.

Respectfully,

Supervising Architect.

W.

Treasury Department,
OFFICE OF THE SUPERVISING ARCHITECT.

Washington, D. C., August 17, 1901.

Sir:

The receipt this day is hereby acknowledged of your communication of the 13th instant, requesting copy of Inspector Packard's report &c., on the work in the building under your charge.

and referring thereto you are informed that the matter will receive due consideration, and action will be taken at the earliest date.

Respectfully,

J. K. TAYLOR,
Supervising Architect.

Treasury Department,
OFFICE OF THE SUPERVISING ARCHITECT.

Washington, D. C., August 17, 1901.

Sir:

The receipt this day is hereby acknowledged of your communication of the 14th instant, requesting authority to purchase coal oil for use at the building under your charge.

and referring thereto you are informed that the matter will receive due consideration, and action will be taken at the earliest date.

Respectfully,

J. K. TAYLOR,
Supervising Architect.

In replying to this Letter the
intials in upper right-hand
corner must be referred to.

TREASURY DEPARTMENT,

OFFICE OF THE SUPERVISING ARCHITECT,

Washington,   August 20, 1901.

Superintendent of Construction,

    U. S. Mint (New),

        Denver, Colo.

Sir:

Your letter of the 24th ultimo has been received and due consideration has been given to the statements contained in the same
and inclosure in relation to defective stone P.14 E., in the exterior walls of the building under your charge.

It is apparent that the contractor has failed to supply a
stone in full accord with the terms of the agreement, but as the
taking out of the stone and replacing it with a new stone might not
be in line with the best interests of the Government at this time,
it is thought that the contractor might be negotiated with with a
view to securing from him a proposal in writing of the amount which
he is willing to deduct from any moneys due him as the cost to him
of removing the present stone and supplying a satisfactory one in
place complete.

You are requested, therefore, to communicate with Mr. J. A.
McIntyre, the contractor, having this end in view, and to submit
with your recommendation such a proposal as has been herein indicated, with the understanding that in the event the same is approved,
he must repair the present stone now in place in a proper and
satisfactory manner.

In compliance with request contained in letter from you dated the 15th instant, there is inclosed herewith copy of report of the 6th instant, made by Mr. A. A. Packard, Inspector of Public Buildings, relative to his examination of this stone and other features of the building.

Respectfully,

Acting Supervising Architect.

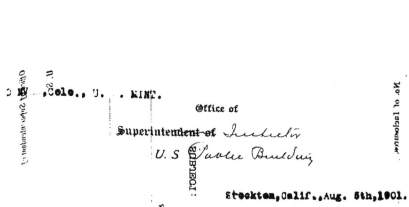

Official Copy Superintendent o

3 MN.,Cole., U. . MINT.

Office of

Superintendent of *Inspector*

U. S *Public Building*

SUBJECT:

Stockton,Calif.,Aug. 5th,1901.

Supervising Architect,

Washington,D. C.

Sir:-

Acting in accordance with instructions in Department letter
S of July 19th,I visited Denver,Colo.,July 29 - Aug. 1st,and
made an inspection of work under contract with Jno. A. McIntyre
for foundations,superstructure and roof covering for the U. .
Mint. At the date of my visit, the work had progresses,as follows:-

BASEMENT:

Practically finished as far as Mr. McIntyre's contract
is concerned, except the fire proofing of some of the steel
columns and the building of two six inch tile short partitions
and the clearing out of rubbish and dirt, to make room for the
cement floor.

FIRST FLOOR:

The work is about complete on this floor,except the
erection of some small six inch tile partitions.

SECOND FLOOR:

The corridor partitions were being erected and there
still remains to be done all of the 6 tile partitions,also some
of the 2nd floor arches have not been put in yet.

ATTIC OR THIRD FLOOR SPACE:

No fire proofing work whatever had been done at the

tíme of my visit.

ROOF:

The deck arches have not been put in; all the other
rough tile work,however, is in place and roof slopes are being
covered with the Spanish tile,all being in place,except about
1/2 of the west slope and 3/4 of the south slope. Some of the
Spanish tile has not been delivered,but is on the way and it
should all be in place by the middle of August. The construct-
ional skylight work is all placed,the copper work,however, has
not been placed,nor has the glass been put in. The cleaning
down and pointing of the stone work still remains to be done,but
I understand work is to commence on that soon . Under ordinary
or normal circumstances, all of the work under Mr. McIntyre's
contract could be finished in 30 days,but judging from the way
the work has, and is progressing, I think it will take fully
two months to clean up all odds and ends in regard to his
contract.

In regard to the character of the work, there is no
doubt but that the Superintendent by his unusually careful
methods has obtained practically a perfect piece of stone work
both as to selection and quality of stone and to the finished
cutting and setting, and the effect throughout is most harmonious.

In regard to the fire proofing, the results are not
as good. In my report of a year ago, I referred to the work
then in place, and stated that a good deal of it was unfit and
should be removed, referring principally to floor arches. Since
that time, more arches have been put in, and where they have
been properly protected, they are in fair shape,although some

that have been put in since my last visit,have commenced to
disintegrate, I would recommend, therefore, that all of the
arches referred to in my report of a year ago as defective,be
removed and replaced by sound tile and all that at the present
time show signs of disintegration be removed and made good.
The partition tile on account of not receiving the effects of the
weather so severely is in better shape although none of it
impresses me as a very good tile, being very unevenly burned,
and showing efflorescence strongly. I imagine that some of the
defective tile may stand the floor tests,which have not been made
yet,but that which has already started to disintegrate may con-
tinue and I doubt whether it will hold the plaster properly and
would therefore recommend that all that shows any signs of
disintegration be removed, and be replaced by sound stuff. On
the exterior, there had appeared at the time of my visit, two
defective stones both being cracked, one in the curbing around
the coal vault and one up near the 2nd story window sill course

determine. At first it appeared to me as though the cement had been worked too rich. I do not think that the making the smaller blocks, as desired by the contractor, would make made, any difference. If carelessness on contractors part either in workmanship or character of material can be established, he should be required to make it good. At the time of my visit there appeared to be a sufficient force of men in proportion to the material on hand to properly carry on the work.

Respectfully,

Allyn A. Packard.

INSPECTOR OF PUBLIC BUILDINGS.

Treasury Department,

OFFICE OF THE SUPERVISING ARCHITECT.

Washington, D.C., August 31, 1901

Superintendent of Construction,

   Mint Building (new),

      Denver, Colorado.

      In view of the request and recommendation contained in your letter of the 14th instant and the public exigency requiring the immediate delivery of the articles and performance of the work you are hereby authorized to incur an expenditure of one dollar and eighty cents ($1.80)

in securing in open market at lowest prevailing rates.

on gallons of coal oil for use in Superintendent's
    office. $ 1.80

      Your attention is called to printed "Instructions to Superintendents," and you will issue and certify vouchers on account of the above in accordance therewith, payment to be made from the appropriation for " Mint Building, Denver, Colorado."

                       Respectfully yours,

                              Acting Chief Executive Officer

Treasury Department.

OFFICE OF THE SUPERVISING ARCHITECT

Washington, D. C., August 21st, 1901.

Mr. Lee Ullery,

Supt. U. S. Mint, Denver, Colo.

Sir:-

I have to acknowledge the receipt of your "Estimate of Funds" required for the work on the building under your superintendence during August, 1901, $258, and to advise you that, as it appears the remittances of funds heretofore made to the Disbursing Agent on account of the appropriation for the building is sufficient to meet all vouchers issued or to be issued for expenditures on account of the work on the building, to and including the last day of the current month, no further remittance will be made to him at present

EB   Respectfully, yours,

Acting Supervising Architect

Treasury Department,
OFFICE OF THE SUPERVISING ARCHITECT,

Washington, D. C., August 22, 1901.

Sir:

The receipt this day is hereby acknowledged of your communication of August 19, 1901, relative to samples for test in connection with building under your charge,

and referring thereto you are informed that the matter will receive due consideration, and action will be taken at the earliest date.

Respectfully,

J. K. TAYLOR,
Supervising Architect.

Treasury Department,
OFFICE OF THE SUPERVISING ARCHITECT,

Washington, D. C., September 21, 1901.

Sir:

The receipt this day is hereby acknowledged of your communication of September 16, 1901, relative to proposal for substitution of certain I beams in bldg., under your charge,

and referring thereto you are informed that the matter will receive due consideration, and action will be taken at the earliest date.

Respectfully,

C. E. KEMPER,
Acting Supervising Architect.

Denver, Colorado, August 27,1901.

Lee Ullery, Esq.,

    Superintendent of Construction, Denver, Colorado.

Sir:-

    Replying to your letter August 23rd, asking for a proposition for reduction on account of imperfection in stone "P-14-E" in the build-ing under your charge, I have the honor to say.

    Being convinced that it will be essential to the acceptance of any proposition, to fully guarantee a perfect and permanent result, the effect to obtain which will cause considerable outlay to me, I desire to offer the following.

    I will drill into said defect, on the upper side of the "swell where the drill marks cannot be seen, and after washing the defect entirely free from drillings so as to insure a perfect bond, force into all openings clear, specially prepared German cement, recutting the face of the stone after the cement has set, and guarantee to the United States that the same shall be absolutely first class in all respects, permanent and indestructible; said guarantee to run for a term satisfactory to the Department, and all work to be subject to your approval.

    In the event of the acceptance of this proposition, I agree to deduct from the total amount of my contract, the sum of Fifty Dollars ($50) without prejudice to the United States of any of its rights in the matter.

               Very respectfully,

                    .(Signed)   J.A.McIntyre,

                        By G.E.Ross-Lewin,Att'y.

JOHN A. McINTYRE,
GENERAL CONTRACTOR,
ROOMS 402-404 COOPER BUILDING,
DENVER, COLO.
Telephone 1238.
OWNER AND OPERATOR
ARKINS GRANITE QUARRIES.

64

Denver Colorado, August 29 1901

Mr Hilary Rah; (

Superintendent Construction.

United States Mint (New) City.

Dear Sir.

I have the honor to acknowledge receipt of your letter
August 23rd. inst. regarding Terra Cotta alledged to be defective.
I shall take the matter up at once with the Terra Cotta Sub
Contractor and advise him of your orders in the matter.

Very Respectfully.

Form No. 175.
Ed. 3 22 1901 8,000.

Treasury Department,

OFFICE OF THE SUPERVISING ARCHITECT,

Washington, D. C.,   July 23, 1901.

Sir:

The receipt this day is hereby acknowledged of your communication of the 20th instant, relative to defective cement covering of coal vault, and enclosing correspondence with contractor relative to same,

and referring thereto you are informed that the matter will receive due consideration, and action will be taken at the earliest date.

Respectfully,

J. K. TAYLOR,
Supervising Architect.

Treasury Department,

OFFICE OF THE SECRETARY,

Aug 26 , 1901

Sir:

The carbon paper referred to in your memorandum of the 23d inst. will be sent you by mail, this day,

Respectfully,

CHIEF OF DIVISION OF STATIONERY, PRINTING, AND BLANKS

...rintendent of Construction,
    New Mint Building,
        Denver, Colorado.

...:

    Referring to your letter of the ... writing and ...
bags of red Diamond Portland cement, forwarded by you
...rial delivered ... ...
... contractors, which you wrote is to be used for ...

    ...nish coat over ... vault, you are advised that ...
is been tested and both the physical and chemical tests
indicate the material to be of excellent quality, and it
is believed that if properly placed the results will be ...
satisfactory.

            Respectfully,

DENVER,COLO.,NEW MINT.

ENCLOSURE 6968.

In replying to this letter the
initials in the upper right-hand
corner must be referred to.

TREASURY DEPARTMENT,

OFFICE OF THE SUPERVISING ARCHITECT.

Washington, September 6, 1901.

Superintendent of Construction,
New Mint Building,
Denver, Colorado.

Sir:

I enclose herewith, for your information and the files
of your office, a copy of Department letter of even date, accepting the proposal of Mr. John A McIntyre, contractor for
the foundation, superstructure and roof covering of the building in your charge, to deduct the sum of fifty dollars ($50.00),
from the amount to be paid him under his said contract, on
account of being allowed to make good certain imperfections
in stone "P-14-E", instead of removing same and substituting
a sound stone therefor, all as stated in detail in said letter
of acceptance, which explains itself.

Respectfully,

Supervising Architect.

M.T.R.

September 9, 1901.

Mr. John A. McIntyre,
    Cooper Building,
        Denver, Colorado.

Sir:

In view of the statements and recommendation contained
in letter of August 26, 1901, from the Superintendent of Construction of the new Mint building at Denver, Colorado, your
proposal, addressed to him, dated August 27, 1901, is hereby
accepted to deduct the sum of fifty dollars ($50.00) from the
amount to be paid you under your contract, dated March 29,1898,
for the foundation, superstructure and roof covering of the
said building, on account of being allowed to repair the break
in stone "P-145N", guaranteeing the permanency of said repairs,
in lieu of removing the same and substituting a sound stone
therefor, in accordance with the terms of your said proposal
and to the full satisfaction of the Superintendent, the amount
being deemed reasonable and a public exigency requiring this
change in the work.

It is understood and agreed that this deduction is not to
affect the time for the completion of the entire work as fixed
in the original contract; that the same is without prejudice to
any and all rights of the United States thereunder; and without
prejudice, also, to the rights of the United States against
the sureties on the bond executed for the faithful fulfillment
of the contract. Please promptly acknowledge the receipt of this letter.
                    Respectfully,

                            Acting Secretary.

B.
J.Q.P.
W.T.R.

DENVER. MINT.

MGD

TREASURY DEPARTMENT,

OFFICE OF THE SUPERVISING ARCHITECT,

Washington, September 10, 1901.

65

The Superintendent of Construction,

U. S. Mint,

Denver, Col.

Sir:

Referring to office letter of yesterday enclosing copy of
Department letter of same day accepting proposal of John A. Mc-
Intyre, contractor for the erection of the building under your
charge, in relation to deducting the sum of $50.00 upon condition
of being allowed to make good certain imperfections in stone
P-14-E, you are now further advised in relation thereto.

The stone must be carefully repaired in a workmanlike manner,
and the cement and pulverized granite used in filling the crack
must not be too wet, and the margins of the crack must be carefully cleaned with water and brush while the pointing is being done,
and before the cement has time to set on the surface.

Respectfully,

Supervising Architect.

DENVER,COLO.,NEW MINT.

TREASURY DEPARTMENT,

OFFICE OF THE SUPERVISING ARCHITECT,

Washington, **September 12,1901.**

Superintendent of Construction,
    New Mint,
        Denver, Colorado.

Sir:

I have to acknowledge the receipt of your letter of the 3rd instant, in which you ask whether the present contractor is under obligation to cover with terra cotta the beams of mezzanine floor forming the framework for ceiling lights over transfer room and coiners room in the first story; also,the beams and girders of attic floor framing, forming the frame work for the large ceiling light between columns Nos.13, 17, 32 and 35, and you are advised that in the opinion of this Office it is not an obligation of the present contractor to place the fireproofing above referred to.

Respectfully,

Supervising Architect.

M.T.R.

Denver, Colo., September 5th, 1901.

Lee Ullery, Esq.,

Superintendent of Construction,

Denver, Colorado.

Sir :-

Referring to our conversation of some days ago regarding eight 6" I-beams required for attic of U.S.Mint building, I ascertain the following:

Said beams not being shown on the "Framing Plans" of the plans sent out by the Department were overlooked by the Gillette-Herzog Mfg.Co., and their shortage was not discovered by me when checking over their entire shipment prior to a final settlement with them last August.

These beams at the contract price with the Gillette-Herzog Company would cost $50.00 but as I have made final settlement with them, I have no option but to pay for same myself in addition to the contract price.

I have been endeavoring to obtain the 6" I's for some time, but am to-day notified by the agent for the American Steel Co., that on account of the strike no 6" "I" can be secured for from six to eight weeks from this date.

I find I can secure 4" "I's" of the required length for the sum of $67.90 which price though excessive, is caused by the strike referred to and entails a net loss to me over and above the contract price of $17.90.

Rather than delay the work I would respectfully ask leave to substitute 4" for the 6" "I" specified, and under the circumstances trust that I may be allowed to make such substitution without further deduction from the contract price.

Very Respectfully,

Treasury Department,

OFFICE OF THE SUPERVISING ARCHITECT.

Washington, D. C.,   9/18/01

Sir: The receipt this day is hereby acknowledged of your communication of   12th, req. authority to expend $9,

and referring thereto you are informed that the matter will receive due consideration, and action will be taken at the earliest date.   Respectfully,

J. K. TAYLOR,
Supervising Architect.

Treasury Department,

OFFICE OF THE SUPERVISING ARCHITECT.

Washington, D. C.,   August 31,1901.

Sir: The receipt this day is hereby acknowledged of your communication of   August 28, 1901, relative to proposal for deduction of $50.00 to repair stone in connection with new Mint building at Denver, Colorado,

and referring thereto you are informed that the matter will receive due consideration, and action will be taken at the earliest date.

Respectfully,

J. K. TAYLOR,
Supervising Architect.

DENVER, NEW MINT.

In replying to this letter the initials and number of the corner must be referred to.

TREASURY DEPARTMENT,

OFFICE OF THE SUPERVISING ARCHITECT,

Washington, September 25, 1901.

Superintendent of Construction,
    New Mint,
        Denver, Colorado.

Sir:

    Referring further to your letter of the 16th instant
enclosing proposal from the contractor for the foundation,
superstructure, etc., of the building under your charge
to substitute 4" I beams for 6" I beams extending from attic
floor framing to roof framing, forming reinforcements of
piers between the window openings "B" of the attic story,
you are directed to reject the proposal as terra cotta wall
to be stiffened is 6" thick, and it is believed that the
stiffening beams should be of the same thickness.

        Respectfully,

        Acting Supervising Architect.

H.M.

AUTHORITY FOR OPEN-MARKET PURCHASE.

'All letters in reply to official communications must refer to initial in upper right hand corner.'

Treasury Department,

OFFICE OF THE SUPERVISING ARCHITECT,

Washington, D. C., **September 23, 1901.**

The Superintendent of Construction,

        U. S. Mint (New),

            Denver, Col.

    Sir:

      In view of the request and recommendation contained in your letter of the **12th inst.,** and the public exigency requiring the immediate delivery of the articles and performance of the work **you are hereby authorized to incur a liability not exceeding fourteen dollars** - **$14.00**

in securing in open market at lowest prevailing rates:

Two tons of coal (2240 lbs. each) for use in your office,	9.00
Two photographic views showing progress of work on the building under your charge, to be taken Sept. 30, 1901,	5.00

      Your attention is called to printed "Instructions to Superintendents," and you will issue and certify vouchers on account of the above in accordance therewith, **charged against the appropriation for the building.**

                Respectfully,

B.

                              Acting Chief Executive Officer.

DENVER, NEW MINT.

TREASURY DEPARTMENT,

OFFICE OF THE SUPERVISING ARCHITECT,

Washington, October 5, 1901.

The Superintendent of Construction,

     U. S. Mint (New),

          Denver, Col.

Sir:

It is the purpose of this office to place on the market at an early day invitations for proposals for the supply of interior finish for the building under your charge.

It is necessary, therefore, that all work embraced in a contract with J. A. McIntyre and Company should be completed without further delay, and you are requested to advise this office what work is as yet incomplete which would prove an obstacle in the performance of work incident to the supply of the interior finish.

It would seem that the matter of correcting defects in floor arches should be settled and this work placed in satisfactory condition, and you are requested to advise this office clearly upon this point, and to make demand upon the contractor for such further work as may be necessary in that direction.

          Respectfully,

                    Acting Supervising Architect.

TREASURY DEPARTMENT,

OFFICE OF THE SUPERVISING ARCHITECT

Washington, **October 7, 1901.**

Superintendent of Construction,
        U.S.Mint,
            Denver, Colo.

Sir:-

        You are advised that the proposals for revolving storm doors,
painting, etc., at the Post Office and Court House building in your
city, have been rejected on account of the informality of the lowest bid, and there being some doubt as to the expediency of authorizing the large expenditure entailed by the installation of the
revolving doors.

        The Custodian has been authorized to solicit new proposals,
however, for the revolving doors and to take alternate bids for
ordinary storm shed enclosures. You are requested to assist him in
the preparation of plans and specifications for these enclosures,
and in securing proposals for the work.

                        Respectfully,

                        Acting Supervising Architect.

Denver, Colo., October 15th, 1901.

Lee Ullery, Esq.,

    Superintendent New Mint,

        Denver, Colorado.

Sir:-

    Replying to your letter October 8th, referring to delay in completion of terra cotta work, I have the honor to hand you herewith tracings of two methods of girder covering submitted for your approval together with copy of letter this day received from the Griffin Clay Manufacturing Company.

            Denver,Colo.,October 12th,1901.

J.A.McIntyre,Esq.,
    City.
Dear Sir:-
    In answer to yours of the 12th instant, giving copy of letter received by you from the Superintendent of Construction of New Mint Building,city, I will state as follows:
    I have on hand enough partition tile to finish all of the different partitions called for in the original contract. Have ordered sufficient arch tile to complete the new arches not in place at present. This arch tile I expect during the coming week; it is my intention to have the bulk of the partitions doe or built up,next week (practically all above basement). The floor arches that remain unset it will take about (not more than) two days to place. As regards the girder covering I am making sketches which you shall have Monday. The tile for this work can be had on short notice. I have placed on one additional tile setter and made arrangements to put on another Next Monday.
    As regards taking out condemned tile, have been working on this part of the work very steadily this week,and expect to have it finished by next Thursday,when Mr.Ullery and myself can go over the parts left and come to some understanding. The tile for this work we have on hand at our factory and there should be no delay in shipping and replacing the parts taken out. Permit me to state that we have

before us 13 full working days before the first of next month in which length of time we can do all of the work required by contract, and some of the replacing of arch tile. I do not see why Mr.Ullery should contemplate withholding an estimate on account of our part of the contract or work as the Government is amply protected by the 10% withheld by it on account of the monthly estimates.

Very truly,

J.R.Kallal, Supt.

This letter is in itself explanatory of all the questions asked in your said letter of the 8th, and I trust same may be satisfactory.

Very respectfully,

(Signed) J.A.McIntyre

by

G.E.Ross-Lewin, Att'y.

DENVER. U.S.MINT.

S.

Superintendent of Construction,

    U.S.Mint,

       Denver, Colorado.

Sir:-

    You are advised that the Custodian of the U.S.Assay Office in
your city,has been this day authorized to incur an expenditure not
to exceed fifty dollars ($50.00),for repairs to the sidewalks
around that building. He has asked that you be instructed to
supervise the work,and you are now requested to advise with and
aid him in the direction of the same.

       Respectfully,

            Supervising Architect.

TREASURY DEPARTMENT,

Inclosure 3890. OFFICE OF THE SUPERVISING ARCHITECT,

Washington,

October 15, 1901.

Superintendent of Construction,

    U. S. Mint (New),

        Denver, Colo.

Sir:

Your letter of the 8th instant is received in relation to the completion of work embraced in a contract with Mr. J. A. McIntyre for the foundations, superstructure, etc., of the building under your charge.

A communication has this day been addressed to Mr. G. E. Ross-Lewin, as the contractor's representative, calling his attention to the backward condition of the work and the causes for the same, and requesting that action be taken to insure early completion.

Regarding terra cotta arches, you are informed that this office desires the best material and workmanship practicable in the construction of the same, and your attention is invited to a letter addressed to you on July 10th, last, in which you were requested not to permit any of these arches to remain where the integrity of the same is at all in question. This applies as well to the disintegration and crumbling of the blocks reported by you as to the ability of the arches to carry loads placed upon them during tests.

Respectfully,

Supervising Architect.

TREASURY DEPARTMENT,
OFFICE OF THE SUPERVISING ARCHITECT.

Washington,
October 16, 1901.

Superintendent of Construction,

   U. S. Mint (New),

     Denver, Colo.

Sir:

    In connection with office letter addressed to you yesterday, you are informed that the communication referred to was not sent to Mr. Ross-Lewin, nor was any other. Please destroy the inclosure sent to you.

    It is requested, however, that you will confer with Mr. Ross-Lewin, advising him, as intimated by you to this office, that the work on the building under your charge is being needlessly delayed by salaried employes under the direction of the contractor, and requesting him to give this matter his attention with a view to the more rapid prosecution of the work, and correction of defects.

        Respectfully,

                    Supervising Architect.

(FORWARDING)

TREASURY DEPARTMENT

OFFICE OF THE SUPERVISING ARCHITECT

Washington, October 21,1901.

The Superintendent of Construction,

New United States Mint,

Denver, Colorado.

Sir:

I am in receipt of your letter of the 15th instant,with enclosure from Mr. J.A. McIntyre,contractor
for the building under your charge,submitting sketches
showing method of fire-proofing of girders under his
contract,and,in reply,I have to advise you that either
method indicated by the sketches submitted will be
satisfactory to this Office.

Prints from the drawings have been prepared,and,
there are this day forwarded to you ,under seperate
cover,duplicate copies,one being for your information
and files and the other for delivery to the contractor.

Respectfully,

Supervising Architect.

P.

RECEIVED at 1114 to 1118 17th St., Denver, Colo.   NEVER CLOSED.

112 A UT AR 29 paid GOVT

Washington, D.C., Oct., 26, 9o1.   562

Supt., Ullery

   Mint, DENVER Colo.

See district Attorney whitford on

the Leach case before starting

for Pueblo as under instructions

twenty fourth instant Answer.

    J.K.Taylor, Supervising Architect

RECEIVED at 1114 to 1118 17th St., Denver, Colo.   NEVER CLOSED.

162 A WI AR 24 paid Govt.

Washington, D.C., Oct., 28, 1901   676

Superintendent Ullery,

   Mint, DENVER. Colo.

Copy of leachs contract on

Pueblo custodians files answer when

you get to Pueblo

   J.K.Taylor ,

     Supervising Architect

     257

Oct 29 1907

Lee Ullery Esq.

Superintendent USM.

Dear Sir.

In reply to your letter Oct 28.

I left off on finishing Mint job because I found caps of
cut off to Water pipes some distance under walk I told
one of their inspectors about it he said he would attend to it
I waited several days for him and then bought pipe connection
so as to make the "Caps" reach to top of flagging.

As to Cementing. I had other cementing to do on Carter,
River, Co Building and left it so as to do both at the
same time which was monday Oct 27

If you want more of the broke broken off Corners
of flagstones taken out and filled with cement I will
most cheerfully do, Mr Lynch called me in to sign a
warrant, but even if I had been paid I would be
willing any time after that to put the job to
a satisfactory finish and to comply with your
instructions. Most Respecfully Yours

L Kindgoetter.

Mr: Ullery:

I have to advise you that the replacing of broken sid..
in the Mint pavement has not begun, and that work has beem completed upon a good many such pavements hereabout.

Respectfully yours,

J. L Hodges

Assayer in Charge.

Lee Ullery, Esq.,

Supt Construction, Mint Bldg.

West Colfax & Evans Streets,

City.

TREASURY DEPARTMENT

OFFICE OF THE SECRETARY

Washington, **October 24, 1901.**

821

The Superintendent of Construction,

    U. S. Mint (New),

        Denver, Col.

Sir:

You are hereby directed to visit, when your duties will permit, the U. S. Post Office at Pueblo, Col., Mr. J. H. Mitchell, Custodian, in relation to matters incident to repairs and painting at the building named, the installation of storm doors, etc.

The said matters are referred to in the enclosed original communications from the Custodian, of the following dates: October 22, 1900, August 10, 1901, August 30, 1901, and October 5, 1901.

The proposals for repairs and painting, supply of revolving doors, etc., have been rejected for the reason that certain complications have arisen as to the extent and meaning of the specification governing the work, and your attention is especially called to the letters of the Custodian now enclosed, and also to letter addressed to him this day by the Supervising Architect of this Department. As soon as you have finished with the enclosures you are directed to return them accompanied by a report addressed to the Supervising Architect, submitting such recommendations as may, in your judgment, be in line with the best interests of the Government. In the event that any work is suggested by you you are requested to prepare a specification therefor, and submit same for approval or amplification before securing competitive bids.

In preparing the specification it is suggested that the items be segregated so that bids may be secured separately for certain branches of work, if so desired.

In regard to the erection of vestibule, as provided for in proposal of the Newton Lumber Company, you are requested, should your judgment be that the proposal is reasonable and that the work should be performed, to submit by wire your recommendation, and to forward the proposal immediately by mail, accompanied by a statement, in writing, from the firm named, to the effect that they will abide by their bid.

The office of the Supervising Architect has been informed, through the Solicitor of the Treasury, that your services may be necessary as a witness in the case of the United States v. L. L. Leach and Son, contractors for the erection of the U. S. Post Office, Pueblo, Col.,and you are requested not to start for that city within three days of the receipt of this communication, so that, if so desired, you may be communicated with in care of the Custodian of the building named.

Your actual traveling and subsistence expenses from Denver to Pueblo, Col., and return, will be paid from an appropriation under the control of the Supervising Architect.

Respectfully,

H. A. Taylor
Assistant Secretary.

S:
T.

PUEBLO.

TREASURY DEPARTMENT

OFFICE OF THE SECRETARY

Washington, October 26, 1901.

Mr. Lee Ullery,

 (Superintendent of Construction, Mint, Denver, Colo.,)

  Care, Custodian, Post Office, Pueblo, Colo.

Sir:

 Referring to Department letter of the 24th instant, directing you to visit the U.S. Post Office building at Pueblo, Colo.
and to an intimation therein that your services might be further desired in connection with the case of U.S. versus L.L.
Leach and Son, contractors for the erection of the U.S.Post Office in the city named, you are now further advised in regard
thereto.

 The Supervising Architect of this Department has by wire
this day, addressed to you at Denver, Colo., requested you before leaving that point to call upon Mr. Greeley W. Whitford, U.S
District Attorney, for conference.

 It is believed that as the result of such conference you
will be fully advised as to the information desired in connection with the case, and you are now requested to make a careful
examination of the Post Office building at Pueblo, and to determine and report the points at which departures have been
made from the requirements of the contract as illustrated by
drawings and governed by specifications.

 In the event that your examination discloses the fact

that changes have been made in the work you are requested to estimate the difference in cost between the work supplied and that required by the contract.

Information has been received that Mr. Charles P. Morrison, Assistant District Attorney has called upon you in regard to matters now the subject of this communication.

Your attention is especially called to the matter of area walls around the building and it is desired that it should be established as to whether the foundation of these walls was laid as governed by the specification. You are requested to make an investigation on this point and to endeavor to ascertain whether the work was performed as agreed upon. Some expense may be incident to pursuing this enquiry and you are authorized to incur a liability of not exceeding thirty dollars ($30.00) in employment of necessary labor &c., and you are requested to forward bills therefor through the Custodian of the building.

Please submit to the office of the Supervising Architect of this Department a report in writing as to the result of your investigations, and you should retain and collect such data as may be of service to you in the event that you are summoned as a witness in the case.

Department letter of the 24th instant,which provided for the payment of your actual traveling and subsistence expenses from Denver, to Pueblo, Colo., and return,is now amplified by

- -

authorizing the payment of any additional subsistence expenses
while in Pueblo in connection with the instructions now given.

Respectfully,

(Assistant Secretary.

S
T

Inclosure 3991.

October 29, 1901.

Mr. Lee Ullery,

C/o Custodian, Post Office,

Pueblo, Colo.

Sir:

This office has learned that certain papers addressed to Mr. Sidney H. Nealy are in the safe of the District Attorney in Chicago, Ill., in connection with the case of the United States vs. L. L. Leach & Son. The District Attorney has been wired this day to re-address the package to you, care of the Custodian of the Post Office at Pueblo, Colo., and in this connection it is proper that you should have the inclosed copy of a report submitted by Mr. Nealy on this subject under date of December 21, 1900.

As soon as you have finished with the papers which may be forwarded by the District Attorney as requested, please carefully re-pack them and return them to him under cover of a letter, in order that they may be fully identified and traced if necessary.

Respectfully,

Supervising Architect.

DENVER, NEW MINT.

In replying to this Letter the
initials in upper right-hand
corner must be referred to.

TREASURY DEPARTMENT

OFFICE OF THE SUPERVISING ARCHITECT

Washington, November 2,1901.

The Superintendent of Construction,

   United States Mint,

      Denver,Colorado.

Sir:

    I have to request that you advise this Office
whether the soil of site for the building of which
you are the Superintendent of Construction is wet
at a depth of 12' below basement floor level.

                    Respectfully,

                    Supervising Architect.

   B.

Washington,   November 5, 1901.

In replying to this Letter the initials in upper right-hand corner must be referred to.

ENCLOSURE

The Superintendent of Construction,

    U.S.   Mint Building,

        Denver, Colorado.

Sir:

    With this there has been forwarded to you a supply of blanks for semi-monthly report of work at the building under your charge. The semi-monthly reports must be submitted on the form indicated, and must be written and <u>mailed</u> on the 15th and last day of each month. In cases where these dates may fall upon a Sunday, they must be written and mailed on the Saturday. There is enclosed a supposititious semi-monthly report for the purpose of informing you as to the scheme, and while it is recognized that in some cases a slight modification may be necessary, adapted to the conditions, it is believed that the method now adopted will apply generally.

    On the sample form the words and statement in purple are those which would be supplied by the Superintendent in charge of the work.

        Respectfully,

                    Supervising Architect .

Completed	. . . . . .	Not commen
Completed	PLUMBING.	Not commen
None	GAS-PIPING.	Not commen
Completed	GLAZING	Not commen
75% completed	PAINTING.	Not commen
20% completed	VAULTS.	Not commen
75% completed	APPROACHES.	Not commen
Not commenced	HEATING,	By contrac force
Not commenced	ELECTRIC WIRING,	No contrac force
	ELEVATORS.	No contrac force
	GENERAL REMARKS:	No contrac force.

...cation from the Office Supervising Architec
of the approval of the following samples:
...ills; butts; leaded roof tile; metal clips.

...has been received of approval of shop draw
metal work.

...ral conduct of the work by the contractor is
unsatisfactory); the delivery of materials a
is adequate (or inadequate) to ensure compl
...ract time. Number of mechanics employed,5
...-setters; 2 brick-layers.

...ing is now up to line of second story linte

Respectfully.

Harvey McDowell,
Superintendent.

O. E. PAGIN,
C. J. TISDEL,
C. B. MORRISON,
BENJAMIN DAVIS,
Asst. U. S. Attorneys.
E. M. FRANKLIN,
Clerk to U. S. Attorney.

H. BETHEA,
U. S. Attorney.

Department of Justice.

OFFICE OF UNITED STATES ATTORNEY
NORTHERN DISTRICT OF ILLINOIS,
537 MONADNOCK BLOCK,
CHICAGO.

Nov. 12, 1901.

Mr. Lee Ullery,

Supt. of Construction U. S. Mint,

Denver, Col.

Dear Sir,-

I beg leave to acknowledge receipt of your favor of
the 9th inst. and also to acknowledge the receipt of the drawings
and specifications forwarded by you in the Leach matter.

Yours very truly,

S. H. Bethea

U. S. Attorney.

The Superintendent of Construction,

Mint Building. (New),

Denver. Colorado.

Sir.

In .... you are hereby authorised to incur an expenditure of eight dollars and fifty five cents ($8.55)

water rate for six months from November 1st.1901, $ 6.75
ten gallons of coal oil for use in Superintendent's
office.   1.80

Inclosure 6678 TREASURY DEPARTMENT,

OFFICE OF THE SUPERVISING ARCHITECT,

In replying to this Letter the initials in upper right-hand corner must be referred to.

Washington, November 15, 1901.

Mr. Lee Ullery,

Superintendent of Construction,

U. S. Mint, New,

Denver, Colo.

Sir:

Under date of the 8th instant the Custodian of the Post Office and Court House at Denver, Colo., was informed that in accordance with Departmental approval, proposals for the supply of revolving doors, etc., were rejected; and you are requested to call at the building and to peruse the letter referred to and to aid the Custodian in such manner as he may desire.

There is now inclosed, as intimated in the foregoing letter, a pencil sketch showing proposed storm inclosures in the lobby on 16th and Arapahoe Streets. While the method suggested is substantially that which is desired, the scheme may possibly be modified in some slight particulars by inclosing two doors on Arapahoe Street and one door on Sixteenth Street.

You are requested, therefore, to give the matter your careful consideration. Should it be necessary, modify in red in slight particulars the scheme now inclosed, and then prepare a specification, and, through the Custodian of the building, invite, by circular letter, proposals for the work.

A copy of this communication has been forwarded to the

- -

Custodian requesting him to set a date for opening bids and to forward them to this office with his recommendation, when immediate action will be taken. Please join with the Custodian in his recommendation.

Respectfully,

Supervising Architect.

Form No. 154. }
Ed. 4 29 1901 1,000. }

NOTICE TO SUPERINTENDENT THAT NO FUNDS WILL BE REMITTED TO DISBURSING AGENT.

Treasury Department,

OFFICE OF THE SUPERVISING ARCHITECT.

Washington, D. C., November 14, 1901.

Superintendent of Construction,

    Mint Building,

        Denver, Colorado.

Sir:

    I have to acknowledge the receipt of your Estimate of Funds required for the work on the building under your superintendence during the month of November   , 1901, and to advise you that, as it appears the remittance of funds heretofore made to the Disbursing Agent is sufficient to meet all vouchers issued or to be issued for expenditures on account of the work, to and including the last day of the current month, no further remittance will be made to him at present.

                  Respectfully,

                             Chief Executive Officer.

H.G.

Office of Custodian,

U. S. Court-House and Post-Office.

PUEBLO, COLO.

Nov. 18th, 1901.

Mr. Lee Ullery,
    Supervising Ard. &c
        Denver, Colo.

My dear Sir;

    The figures of Mr. J. C. Summers
on concrete work asked for by you
in your letter of yesterday are;
"New side walks, area floors & portions
  of street curb & resetting street curbs, using
  concrete as per specifications $1,329.80 "

Basement floor, as per Specification $2,634.50.

    Yours very Truly,
        Jn? H. Mitchell.
          Custodian.

(PRINTED HEADING).

Denver,Colorado,November 12th,1901.

Lee Ullery,Esq.,

    Superintendent Construction,

        Denver Mint, Denver, Colorado.

Sir:-

    Referring to your letter November 11th,1901, directing me to remove certain cracked and broken tile in the roof covering of the United States Mint Building this city, under your charge, and substitute therefor sound tile in accordance with the approved sample, I have the honor to say:

    Each and every tile placed in said roof (including those complained of) was personally inspected by you and duly approved, and all work done in the construction of said roof was also inspected and approved by you,as in full accordance with the specification,for said building.

    When one of the cracks complained of first materialized,fearing that I was to blame,I at once removed all broken tile and replaced same with perfect material,since which time other and additional cracks have appeared,of which you now complain.

    I am informed and believe that you advised my representative Scott Truxtun in a conversation had with him regarding the matter of the broken tile "you (Truxtun) are not to blame in the matter, and I doubt if you can be held for it", also, that you requested Truxtun to give you a bid for repairing said roof and guarantee it for one year.

I have consulted the best authorities obtainable in the matter and after a careful examination of the methods of construction pursued am forced to say that I consider the breakage of the tile referred to as wholly the result of defective construction (no allowance having been made for expansion and contraction) and that the same is not in any way chargeable to me.

I therefore,respectfully decline to comply with the demands contained in your said letter of November 11th,instant,and appeal from your decision to the Supervising Architect.

Very respectfully,

(Signed) John A.McIntyre,

By G.E.Ross-Lewin.

(PRINTED HEADING).

Denver, Colo., November 12th,1901.

'e Ullery, Esq.,

  Superintendent of Construction,

    Denver Mint, Denver, Colorado.

Sir:-

  Referring to your letter Nov.11th,1901, directing me to remove certain broken glass in the skylight of the United States Mint building, this city, under your charge, and substitute new glass therefor, I have the honor to say:

  I am informed and believe that you personally inspected each light of glass before same was placed in position, and passed upon its quality,but, that you insisted that all of said glass be fitted tight, so as to prevent leakage,as you had determined that "THIS skylight,should not leak at all", although the foreman in charge of the work cautioned you against said method,advising that a certain play be left for expansion and contraction,but, that you personally,and at all times, directed the work,and insisted that the same be conducted in accordance with your directions.

  I therefore respectfully decline to comply with the instructions contained in your said letter Nov.11.inst. and appeal from your decision to the Supervising Architect.

     Very respectfully,

      (Signed) John A.McIntyre
      By G.E.Ross-Lewin.

Denver,Colo.,November 22nd,1901

Lee Ullery,Esq.,

       Superintendent of Construction

          Denver Mint (New), Denver, Colorado.

Sir:-

       I have the honor to advise you that on November 20th, 1901, the Griffin Clay Manufacturing Company abandoned their contract upon the terra cotta work of the United States Mint building under your charge,and ceased work thereon; That on November 21st,1901, there was served upon them the eight day notice provid -ed for in their said contract, and that upon the expiration of said time the work will be promptly resumed and the same pushed to immediate completion.

          Very respectfully,

          (Signed J.A.McIntyre,

             Per Geo.E.Ross-Lewin,

                 Atty.
                  T.

JOHN A. MCINTYRE,
GENERAL CONTRACTOR,
ROOMS 402-401 COOPER BUILDING,
DENVER, COLO.
Telephone 1238.
OWNER AND OPERATOR
ARKINS GRANITE QUARRIES.

Denver, Colo., Nov. 22, 1901.

Lee Ullery Esq.,

    Supt. Construction,

      U. S. Mint (New) Denver Colo.

        Sir.

        I have the honor to acknowledge receipt of your letter November 19.inst. relating to certain broken stone in the walls of the U. S. Mint Building this city under your charge, and in reply thereto have the honor to say; The location and peculiar character of the cracks in the stone referred to, when considered in connection with the painstaking manner of laying, and the extreme care taken in the inspection thereof, convince me that the breaks referred to are in no way chargeable either to defective material or workmanship, but rather to some inherent defect in the construction itself.

I would therefor respectfully request that I be allowed to hold the matter in abeyance for a few days in order that I may have time in which to prepare a specific statement of the matter as it appears to me.

      Very Respectfully.

        J A McIntyre
        Per Geo E Ross

DENVER, NEW MINT

(INCLOSURE 6057)

TREASURY DEPARTMENT,

OFFICE OF THE SUPERVISING ARCHITECT

Washington, November 21, 1901.

Superintendent of Construction,

Branch Mint (new),

Denver, Colorado.

Sir:

Please fill out, carefully, the enclosed blanks relative
to electric lighting, power, gas and telephone companies in
Denver, and return the same to this office as soon as possible.

Respectfully,

Supervising Architect.

SBP

Treasury Department,

OFFICE OF THE SUPERVISING ARCHITECT.

Washington, D. C., November 22, 1901.

Sir:
    The receipt this day is hereby acknowledged of your communi-
cation of the 19th instant, relative to broken glass in skylight and defective Spanish tiles on roof of the building under
your charge,
and referring thereto you are informed that the matter will
receive due consideration, and action will be taken at the
earliest date.

Respectfully,

J. K. TAYLOR,
Supervising Architect.

IN A. McINTYRE,
GENERAL CONTRACTOR.
82-404 COOPER BUILDING,
DENVER, COLO.
Telephone 1238.

OWNER AND OPERATOR
% GRANITE QUARRIES.

98

Denver Colorado. Nov. 30 1901.

Lee Ullery Esq.

    Superintendent U. S. Mint (New)

        Denver   Colorado.

Sir.

    Referring to your letter 19th. inst. calling my attention
to certain cracked stone in the United States Mint Building under
your charge, and requesting me to make some proposition to the
Department looking towards the remedy of the same, I have the
honor to hand you, herewith enclosed, a communication to Hon. J.
K. Taylor Supervising Architect, containing a full statement of
the matter as it appears to me.

           Very Respectfully.

               A. McIntyre

               Per

Denver Colo. Nov 20 1902.

Mr. Ellery Esq.

    Superintendent Construction.

       Denver   Colorado.

  Sir,

      Referring to the matter of the stoppage of work on the terra-cotta work of the building under your charge, I have the honor to say that the traffic that may be have will be required thereon, and that the same will be carried to completion, I being assured that the building will be completed no later than December 31st next

        Very respy. yours,

PUEBLO.

TREASURY DEPARTMENT,

OFFICE OF THE SUPERVISING ARCHITECT,

Washington, November 29, 1901.

Enclosure.

Mr. Lee Ullery,

Superintendent of Construction,

U. S. Mint,

Denver, Colorado.

Sir:

I enclose herewith Treasury Draft No. 191805, drawn
in your favor on the Assistant Treasurer of the United States
at Chicago, Illinois, for $44.45
for expenses incurred by you in traveling from Denver, Colorado,
to Pueblo, Colorado, and return.

Respectfully,

Chief Executive Officer.

H.G.

(P R I N T E D   H E A D I N G)

Denver, Colorado, Nov.30, 1901.

Hon. J.K.Taylor,
      Supervising Architect,
         Washington, D.C.

Sir:-

      On November 19th, 1901, Lee Ullery, Esq., Superintendent of Construction of the United States Mint Building (New), this city, by his letter of said date, called my attention to certain cracked stone in said building. i.e.

    "Q-12-E" (below 2nd story sills) Cracked through middle.
    "L-16-E" (below Egg and Dart) Cracked through middle.
    "A-7-W" (above 2nd story sills) cracked at end.
    Window sill Central window "E" side, cracked at end.
    Window sill 2nd. window "S" side, cracked at end.

      These stones in common with all others placed in the building, were subjected to a careful and searching inspection both as to quality and color at the stone yards, prior to cutting, and again at the building after being cut, being again inspected when placed in the wall, the bedding being carefully and evenly done under the personal supervision of your representative.

      I have subjected the stones in question and the building itself, to careful examination by competent engineers, and, am convinced that the defects in question are in no way chargeable to me, or caused by any neglect or oversight on my part.

      I feel that I have at all times shown my willingness to comply with requests of your Department no matter what personal inconvenience, and, in consideration of this fact and the many difficulties experienced in my completion of this contract, would respectfully request that I be allowed to remedy the defects complained of by forcing into the cracks specially prepared German cement, re-cutting the faces of the stone after setting, and guaranteeing a permanent and satisfactory result. All work to be done to the satisfaction of the Superintendent of Construction, and without additional expense to the United States or further deduction from the contract price for said building.

        Very respectfully

        (Signed) John A.McIntyre,
           By Geo.E.Ross-Lewin, Atty.

RECEIVED at 1114 to 1118 17th St., Denver, Colo.

62 A Fw On 16 Paid Gov't

Washington B C Dec 2-01

Clerk to Supt New Mint

Denver Col.   925

Wire Supt Ullerys address.

J K Taylor, Supervising Architect.

240 Pm

7A-BX.HE.SD. 21- Paid. Gov't.

Washington, D.C. Dec 3 rd, 1901

Supt Ullery,

THE WESTERN UNION TELEGRAPH COMPANY.

——— INCORPORATED ———
21,000 OFFICES IN AMERICA.   CABLE SERVICE TO ALL THE WORLD.

RECEIVED at 1114 to 1118 17th St., Denver, Colo.   **NEVER CLOSED.**

21 A UT NR 23 Paid Govt
Washington, DC Dec. 4

Supt. Uller,

New Mint, Denver, Col.

Averill this office will be at Denver on Tuesday
morning Be there.

J K Taylor,

Supervising architect.

914 am

1024

Inclosure 6513.

TREASURY DEPARTMENT,
OFFICE OF THE SUPERVISING ARCHITECT,

Washington,

December 4, 1901.

Superintendent of Construction,

U. S. Mint (New),

Denver, Colo.

Sir:

There is inclosed herewith copy of a communication of the 30th ultimo from Mr. John A. McIntyre, contractor for the erection of the building under your charge, in relation to certain cracked stones to which you had called his attention.

Mr. F. L. Averill of this office will be at the building by next Tuesday, as you have today been advised by wire, and it is requested that you will submit this matter to him and after a conference with him in relation thereto, submit a report to this office with your recommendation in the premises.

Respectfully,

Supervising Architect.

DENVER, NEW MINT.

F

TREASURY DEPARTMENT,

OFFICE OF THE SUPERVISING ARCHITECT,

Washington, December 4, 1901.

The Superintendent of Construction,

    U. S. Mint Building, (new),

        Denver, Colorado.

Sir:

    Referring to the request for leave of absence submitted by Mr. Oscar Hinrichs, Clerk, and recommended by you, you are requested to state, in view of the fact that you have already been granted leave for thirty days, if it is intended for both you and your Clerk to be absent from the building at the same time. No action will be taken in regard to granting the request of Mr. Hinrichs, until receipt of reply from you.

        Respectfully,

            Supervising Architect,

DENVER, NEW MINT.

(FORWARDING)

TREASURY DEPARTMENT,

OFFICE OF THE SUPERVISING ARCHITECT,

Washington, December 5,1901.

106

The Superintendent of Construction,

    United States (new) Mint,

        Denver,Colorado.

Sir:

    There has been forwarded this day to the above
address a set of prints for the interior finish of the
building for which you are the Superintendent of Construction. This package is marked,"For Mr. F.L.Averill,"
but you are requested to open same and examine the drawings so as to become acquainted with them as far as possible prior to the arrival of Mr. Averill at the building.

        Respectfully,

                    Supervising Architect.

B.

JOHN A. MCINTYRE,
GENERAL CONTRACTOR,
402-401 COOPER BUILDING,
DENVER, COLO.
Telephone 1239.
OWNER AND OPERATOR
KINS GRANITE QUARRIES.

Denver Colorado. Dec. 10 1901.

Lee Ullery Esq.

Superintendent Construction.

Denver Colorado.

Sir.

I have the honor to enclose you herewith the certificate
of City Engineer, which I believe is required by the terms of
my contract.

Very Respectfully.

W M Sulyn
By Geo E Rase Lewis
Att'y.

(P R I N T E D   H E A D I N G).

Denver, Colorado, December 9th, 1901.

TO WHOM IT MAY CONCERN:

In order to enable the contractor for the erection of the United States Mint Building, this city, to comply with the terms of his said contract, I, on October 29th, 1901, visited the said Mint building, and after consultation with Lee Ullery, Supt. Constn. thereof, made the following measurements and ascertained the following elevations:

```
Top of Water Table, N.E.corner of building, Elevation 62.570 ft.
 "    "    "     "    S.E.   "          "        "      62.645  "
 "    "    "     "    S.W.   "          "        "      62.560  "
 "    "    "     "    N.W.   "          "        "      62.540  "
Top of Door Sill,Front entrance                 "      62.600  "
Top of Platform,Front entrance steps            "      57.440  "
```

LINE MEASUREMENTS

```
North Face Building,East end to So.line Colfax Ave. 23.00 ft.
North Face Building,West end to So.line Colfax Ave. 22.970 "
```

All measurements in feet and decimals of a foot, and all elevations are distances above the "Official City Datum Planum".

I certify to the correctness of all the above elevations and distances.

Very respectfully,

(Signed) P. O'Brian.

City Engineer, City of Denver.

Original transmitted to Supervising Architect with Superintendent's letter of December 10.19.

RECEIVED at 1114 to 1118 17th St., Denver, Colo.   NEVER CLOSED.

SCH.X.CM. 14 Paid   583

Cheyenne Wyo Dec 10th 1901.

L.Ulley, Supt Construction

New Mint, Denver,Colo.

What date will you be in Cheyenne to inspect stone

for public building answer

Foster & Smith.

131pm

Form No. 175.
Ed. 3 22 1901 6,000.

Treasury Department,
OFFICE OF THE SUPERVISING ARCHITECT.
Washington, D. C., December 9, 1901.

Sir:
The receipt this day is hereby acknowledged of your communi-
nication of the 5th instant, relative to securing photographs
work on the building,

and referring thereto you are informed that the matter will
receive due consideration, and action will be taken at the
earliest date.

Respectfully,

J. K. TAYLOR,
Supervising Architect.

Form No. 40.
FJ 7 26 1901 3,000.

DENVER, NEW MINT.

AUTHORITY FOR OPEN-MARKET PURCHASE.

(All letters in reply to official communications must refer to initial in upper right-hand corner.)

110

S.
P.

P

Treasury Department,

OFFICE OF THE SUPERVISING ARCHITECT,

Washington, D. C., December 10, 1901

Superintendent of Construction,

U. S. Mint Building (new),

Denver, Colorado.

Sir:

In view of the request and recommendation contained in your letter of the 5th instant, and the public exigency requiring the immediate delivery of the articles and performance of the work you are hereby authorized to incur an expenditure not exceeding five dollars ($5.00)

in securing in open market at lowest prevailing rates:

Photographic views of work on the building , $ 5.00

TREASURY DEPARTMENT,   *I I I*

OFFICE OF THE SUPERVISING ARCHITECT,

Washington, December 12, 1901.

The Superintendent of Construction,

    U. S. Mint Building, (new),

        Denver, Colorado.

Sir:

    In view of the statements contained in your letter of the 9th instant, in regard to leave of absence of Mr. Oscar Hinrichs, Clerk, you are hereby authorized to grant the leave on such days as the above named Clerk can be spared from duty, and you are requested to keep a record of the time so granted and at the expiration of the present month to report the same to the office for ratification.

        Respectfully,

                Supervising Architect.

DENVER. P.O.

B

Inclosure No. 6463.

TREASURY DEPARTMENT,

OFFICE OF THE SUPERVISING ARCHITECT,

Washington, December 12, 1901.

W

Superintendent of Construction,

U. S. Mint (New),

Denver, Colorado.

Sir:

There is inclosed herewith for your information copy of office letter of this date addressed to the Custodian of the Post Office and Court House in your city, revoking office letter of the 15th ultimo, advising him with reference to a plan forwarded to you for storm doors at that building. In view of the position now taken by this office, office letter of the 15th ultimo addressed to you on the same subject is also revoked.

Respectfully,

L

J. K. Taylor

Supervising Architect.

5

DENVER. P.O.

 COPY.

B

In replying to this letter the initials in upper right-hand corner must be referred to.

TREASURY DEPARTMENT,

OFFICE OF THE SUPERVISING ARCHITECT.

F
F.A.C.

Washington, December 12, 1901.

an,

U. S. Post Office and Court House,

Denver, Colorado.

Sir:

In view of the objections set forth in your communication
of the 25th ultimo, and the Postmaster's letter of the 21st ultimo
inclosed therewith, office letter of the 15th ultimo with reference
to the plan prepared by this office for storm doors in the building
in your custody, and in which you were advised that the Superintendent of Construction of the U. S. Mint at Denver, had been authorized
to secure proposals for the performance of the work, is hereby revoked;
and as the office declines to reconsider its action in disapproving of
the plans submitted by the Superintendent, the matter of providing new
strom doors will be deferred for this season.

Respectfully,

(Signed)   J. K. Taylor,

Supervising Architect.

L

S

CHEYENNE, WYO., Dec. 14th, 1901.

Mr. Lee Ullery,

Superintendent of Construction,

New Mint, Denver, Colorado.

Sir:-

Your letter of the 13th inst. received in
regard to inspection of quarries.   We think
it can be done at present, as Mr. Clark, foreman
for Keefe & Bradley, came from the Iron Mountain
to-day, and states there is very little snow in
quarries.

We wish you would come as soon as possible,
so we may know what to do.

Respectfully,

Forster A. Smith

The Superintendent of Construction,

    (New) United States Mint,

        Denver, Colorado.

Sir:

    The receipt of your letter of the 20th instant, with enclosure from the City Engineer of Denver, relative to certain elevations of the building for which you are the Superintendent of Construction, is hereby acknowledged, and in reply you are advised that same has been noted and placed on file.

        Respectfully,

                    Supervising Architect.

D.

DENVER.

116 P

Form No. 184.
Ed. 8-29-1901 1,000.

NOTICE TO SUPERINTENDENT THAT NO FUNDS WILL BE REMITTED TO DISBURSING AGENT.

Treasury Department,

OFFICE OF THE SUPERVISING ARCHITECT,

Washington, D. C., December 16, 1901.

Superintendent

    U.S. Mint Building,

       Denver, Col.

Sir:

    I have to acknowledge the receipt of your Estimate of Funds
required for the work on the building under your superintendence
during the month of December , 1901 , and to advise you that,
as it appears the remittance of funds heretofore made to the Disbursing Agent is sufficient to meet all vouchers issued or to be
issued for expenditures on account of the work, to and including
the last day of the current month, no further remittance will be
made to him at present.

                Respectfully,

                                  Chief Executive Officer.

J.H.T.

Mr. Joe Cleary,

        Superintendent of Construction, &c.,

                  St. Louis, Mo.

                  Dear Sir,

        Under date of the 10th instant, Messrs. Fraser and
        ....
        .... Cheyenne Winston, resident in Indian
        on Window would be able to................................
        ....
        ....
        ....

- -

If it is your opinion, after familiarizing yourself with all
the conditions that a sufficient and satisfactory supply of the
stone cannot be obtained from the Iron Mountain quarries, it is
requested that you suggest to the contractors the advisability of
presenting to the Department a proposal, in writing, to substitute
some other stone therefor, that can be secured in ample and satisfactory quantities, and that will meet with the requirements of the
specification; they to accompany their proposition with a sample
of the stone, when further consideration will be given to the matter.

Your report should embrace your recommendations as to the
acceptance of such a proposal, if one is presented.

A portion of the accepted sample of the Iron Mountain sandstone
has been forwarded to the Postmaster at Cheyenne, Wyoming, who is
Custodian of the Site of the building, and may be seen by you upon
request.

Upon completion of the above duties return to Denver, Colorado.

Your actual traveling and subsistence expenses while in the
performance of this duty will be paid from appropriations under the
control of the Supervising Archetect of this Department.

Your departure from Denver, in accordance with the above instructions should be deferred until after the visit of a representative from the Supervising Architect's office, who will be direct-

in a few days to visit the building in your charge, in connection with work under contract.

Please wire date of your leaving Denver, Colorado, for Cheyenne, Wyoming.

Respectfully,

H A Taylor

Assistant Secretary.

M X 22 Paid Govt

Washing ton DC Dec 20th 1901

Lee Al mery, Inter Ocean Hotel

Cheyenne Wyo.

Unnec essary to visit quarries return

to Denver to submit report.

H. A. Taylor acting secy   152PM.

DEN... MINT.
H

*In replying to this Letter the
. ...ials in upper right-hand
corner must be referred to.*

TREASURY DEPARTMENT,

OFFICE OF THE SUPERVISING ARCHITECT,

CIRCULAR LETTER. Washington,   December 21, 1901.

119 s

Superintendent of Construction,

    Mint Building,

        Denver,Colo.

Sir:-

    All orders relating to travelling are conveyed by Department letters,signed by the Honorable, the Assistant Secretary of the Treasury,but acknowledgment of receipt,or reports incident thereto, must be addressed to the Supervising Architect.

    This direction is given for the reason that,in some instances, the acknowledgment of receipt of orders has been addressed to the Honorable Assistant Secretary.

              Respectfully,

              Supervising Architect.

In replying to this letter the initials in upper right-hand corner must be referred to.

TREASURY DEPARTMENT,

OFFICE OF THE SUPERVISING ARCHITECT,

Washington, .

December 28, 1901.

121

TO SUPERINTENDENTS OF CONSTRUCTION AND DISBURSING AGENTS OF

PUBLIC BUILDINGS.

To enable this office to respond to a call for information from Congress, it is absolutely necessary that all vouchers and accounts for the month of December, 1901, should be properly made up and forwarded to the Department immediately after the close of the month. It is essential that no delay should be allowed to supervene in this connection.

Supervising Architect.

In REPLYING TO THIS LETTER THE
INITIALS IN UPPER RIGHT-HAND
CORNER MUST BE REFERRED TO.

TO SUPERINTENDENTS OF CONSTRUCTION OF PUBLIC BUILDINGS.

The accompanying form of pay roll, commencing with
the month of January, 1902, will be used to the exclusion of all
forms now in stock, when submitting accounts covering compensation due the contingent force.   With the exhaustion of those
sent herewith, requisition should be made on this office for an
additional supply of the forms.

Supervising Architect.

CHEYENNE.

Enclosure 7623.

TREASURY DEPARTMENT,

OFFICE OF THE SUPERVISING ARCHITECT.

Washington, January 8, 1902.

/ 23

Mr. Lee Ullery,

 Superintendent of Construction,

  Mint Building,

   Denver, Colorado.

Sir:-

 I enclose herewith Disbursing Clerk George A.
Bartlett's check, No. 192858, drawn to your order, in the sum
of...$24.35,
for expenses incurred by you in traveling from Denver, Colo.,
to Cheyenne, Wyo., and return, under orders from this Department.

 Please acknowledge receipt.

  Respectfully,

     Chief Executive Officer.

FD

Mr.Lee Ullery,
          Superintendent of Construction,
                    U.S.Mint, Denver, Colorado.

Dear Sir :-

          The property owners on Colfax Avenue are trying to get that
street paved from Evans Street,where the paving now ends, to the bridge
across Cherry Creek,but as the Government owns such a large frontage
on Colfax Avenue,Evans and South 13th Streets,it is impossible to pave
unless some provision is made for the Government to pay its proportion
of the cost of paving around the new mint. This would cost probably
from $8,000. to $10,000. and the city has no funds with which to meet
this, so that, unless the Government makes some provision for paying
its proportion of the cost, the paving cannot be done. We think,when
brought to the attention of the proper authorities,there will be no objection to making an appropriation to meet this expense,and thus enable
us to pave these streets,as paving will certainly add very materially
to the appearance of the streets around the new mint besides keeping
the interior of the building free from dust,

          Trusting you will take the matter up with the proper author-
ities and that we may hear from you soon, I remain,

                              Very truly yours,

                                   (Signed) A.T.Harlow.

Department of Justice.
———
OFFICE OF UNITED STATES ATTORNEY
NORTHERN DISTRICT OF ILLINOIS,
537 MONADNOCK BLOCK,
CHICAGO.

O. E. PAGIN,
C. J. TISDEL,
C. B. MORRISON,
BENJAMIN DAVIS,
    Asst. U. S. Attorneys.
E. M. FRANKLIN,
    Clerk to U. S. Attorney.

2

to it, and indicate how I should insert it in the bill.

Thanking you in advance, I am,

Sincerely yours,

C. B. Morrison
Asst, U. S. Attorney.

C. B. M.

Mr, ___ ___ ___,

        ___ ___ ___

Dear Sir:

        The Alloys for ___ ___ as submitted by the gentlemen
introduced to me while at your office, has been given over to
the Assayer at this Mint for testing purposes.

        The Assayers testimony, for, seem to be favorable for
what we in question. If they all give good results I will no
___ to recommend the above mentioned above and would be pleased
receive from you the ___ name to name of ___ from ___.
___ at one she retained.

                        Very truly

                                ___ ___ ___

                        U S ___ ___ ___, Mint, ___ Pa.

———, 190——

Superintendent.

SUBJECT:

In replying to this Letter the
initials in upper right-hand
corner must be referred to.

TREASURY DEPARTMENT,

OFFICE OF THE SUPERVISING ARCHITECT,

Washington, January 20, 1902.

Superintendent of Construction,

U. S. Mint (New),

Denver, Colo.

Sir:

Replying to your communication of the 2d instant suggesting
that you be instructed to visit this office for conference with
draftsmen in connection with the preparation of drawings for the
interior finish of the building under your charge, you are informed
that it is believed there is sufficient data here upon which to
prepare the necessary drawings and specifications for this work,
and the visit suggested is not considered necessary.

Respectfully,

[signature]

Acting Supervising Architect.

TREASURY DEPARTMENT

OFFICE OF THE SECRETARY

Washington, January 20, 1902.

Sir:,
Superintendent of Construction
New Mint.
Denver, Colo.

The Department has the honor to acknowledge the receipt of communication of the 16th instant, addressed to the Supervising Architect, forwarding copies of certain correspondence between your-self Mr. A. T. Sarles, relative to the paving of certain streets the New Mint building at Denver sixth.

reply to that portion of your letter in which you suggest expense of such improvement be borne proportionately by States, you are informed that, by the terms of the bond a will of a site is a deed, the Governor of the State directing the United States exclusive jurisdiction over of the New Mint and the building thereon, it is expressly that said property is "deemed and exempt from all taxation and assessments of every name and nature for and how as the United States shall remain the owner thereof." the foregoing, you are advised that this Department

DENVER,Colo.New Mint, Mr. Ullery--Jan. 20,1902--2

has no appropriation under its control which can be made available
for the payment of assessments for street improvements and the
utmost limit to which this Department can proceed in the way of
expenditures outside of the lot lines is in laying sidewalks and
curbing which, by long-continued practice, have been permitted by
the accounting officers on the theory that they are part of the
approaches to public buildings.

As indicating the views held by the accounting officers of
this Department in reference to expenditures for street improvements from appropriations under the control of this Department,
your attention is invited to the following extract from the opinion rendered under date of September 8, 1897, by the Comptroller of
the Treasury on the question submitted to him whether this Department could legally pay from the appropriation for the Federal building an assessment for sewers levied by the municipal authorities
of the City of New London, Connecticut.

"The facts, as I understand them,are that the city
extended its line of sewers through its own streets or other
property, causing this extension to pass adjacent to the said
Government building and its grounds,and, stripping the demand of the city from all verbage, it is a demand upon the
Government,before it shall be permitted to connect its building and grounds with said extension, to pay to the city the
sum of $195.06, a part of the cost of constructing its own
sewer under its own streets and other property exclusively
owned by the city."

DENVER,Colo, New Mint, Mr. Ullery, Jan. 20, 1902--3

x   x   x   x   x   x   x   x   x

"So far as the Government is concerned, it would be
a payment to a private person for private use of public
money."

"I do not understand that it is contended that there
has been by the accounting officers of the Government
any uniform,contemporaneous,and long-continued construction of these statutes providing for public buildings which would justify a payment out of these appropriations to an individual or city to reimburse them
for the cost of private improvements owned and con-
trolled by them. Such a construction would have prov-
ed disastrous to the interests of the Government,and I
shall not, at this late date, let down the bars by calling an assessment by some other name,thereby paving the
way for such unauthorized expenditures of the public
money, and especially under the terms of this appropriation,guarded in such careful manner as it is."

"If Congress desires to expend public moneys to reimburse cities for the extension of their sewer systems,
making them contiguous to Government property,it is well
and good; but this result should not in general or particular cases be brought about or made possible by ju-
dicial legislation by the Comptroller."

"In this particular case payment of this sum of
money to the city authorities of New London,Conn.,might
and doubtless would be a matter of great convenience
to the Government in order to a speedy occupation and
use of the buildings, but would carry with it the
moral obligation of the Government to reimburse the
many other cities which are constantly knocking at the
doors of Congress for pay for the use and construction of streets and sewers built and constructed by
these cities and used by the Government."

You will please advise Mr. Harlow of the tenor of this letter and
inform him that this Department'cannot take favorable action on

DENVER, Colo. New Mint, Mr.Ullery, Jan. 20, 1902--4

his request.

Respectfully,

Assistant Secretary.

T
WFF

Form No. 184.
Ed.8 29 1901 1,000.

NOTICE TO SUPERINTENDENT THAT NO FUNDS WILL BE REMITTED TO DISBURSING AGENT.

Treasury Department,

OFFICE OF THE SUPERVISING ARCHITECT,

Washington, D. C., January 18, 1902.

Superintendent

U. S. Mint, Denver, Col.

Sir:

I have to acknowledge the receipt of your Estimate of Funds required for the work on the building under your superintendence during the month of January , 1902, and to advise you that, as it appears the remittance of funds heretofore made to the Disbursing Agent is sufficient to meet all vouchers issued or to be issued for expenditures on account of the work, to and including the last day of the current month, no further remittance will be made to him at present.

Respectfully,

Chief Executive Officer.

Lee Ullery Esq
            Supt.
                Denver Colo.

Dear Sir
        I have your favor of this date
concerning stone submitted to

Healey for test.
The stone submitted is from the upper strata
of the "Whinstone Quarries" near the
city of Golden, County of Jefferson and
State of Colorado, owned by The Inter-
State Realty and Contracting Co. with its
principal office in Denver Colorado.
            Very Respectfully
                J. O. Bealey.

Jany 21st, 1902

DENVER, NEW MINT.

S.H.

TREASURY DEPARTMENT,

OFFICE OF THE SUPERVISING ARCHITECT,

Washington,   January 25, 1902.

Enclosure 4923.

Superintendent of Construction,

U. S. Mint (New),

Denver, Colorado.

Sir:

Enclosed herewith find copy of a report submitted to this
office under date of the 21st ultimo, by Mr. F. L. Averill, Structural Engineer, as the result of his visit paid to the building
under your charge.

The report will explain itself.

As recommended in the report, the matter of correcting the
defective Spanish tile on the roof of the building, which formed
the subject of your letters of November 19th last and the 21st
instant, will receive consideration in the specifications for the
interior finish, &c., which are now in course of preparation, as
the contractor is not deemed responsible for the defects.

Referring to your letter of November 19th last, with enclosure, you are advised that the contractor is held responsible for
the broken glass in the skylight and demand should be made by you,
upon him, therefore, to replace the same with glass in accordance
with the terms of the contract.   Your letter of the 21st instant,

in relation to this matter is also received and is hereby acknowledged.

Your attention is now called to your letter of November 22nd
last, in relation to the suspension of the terra cotta work, with
the request that you advise this office whether active operations
have been commenced thereon, or whether the weather conditions have
been suitable to permit of a resumption of this work.

Your letters of the 3rd and 17th ultimo, with enclosures, are
hereby acknowledged, in relation to broken stones in the facing
of the building, together with your communication of the 21st instant on the same subject. Your attention is called to the statements made by Mr. Averill, in regard to this matter, and you are
advised that no objection will be made to your permitting the contractor to repair the stones "Q-12-E" and "L-16-E" and the two window sills in a manner similar to that used in repairing stone "P-
14-E", which formed the subject of the approval of the Department
under date of September 9th last, the contractor to submit through
you a proposal in a reasonable amount for a deduction, if the repairs indicated are allowed to be made. Please forward such proposal, when received, with your specific recommendation, for further action, and permit no repairs on the stone to be made until
the receipt by you of the Department's acceptance of the contract-
or's proposal for the deduction on account thereof.

Stone "A-7-W" and "A-24-S", however, are to be treated as recommended in your letter of the 17th ultimo, by having the fillet ends cut off to the angle, the stone cut out to a depth of 6" from the face and new blocks of granite inserted, matching those now in place, neatly and closely fitted and cemented in place, the cement joint to be on line of present angle of the stone.

The broken piece of marble at top of second story window at south side of building, should be cut, removing the moulded portion, as indicated by the pencil line on the sketch submitted with your letter of the 17th ultimo, to the full depth of the marble and a new piece of marble inserted in lieu thereof, to match the marble in place, jointed in the angle of the marble work, bedded and pointed with mortar of lime and pulverized marble.

This communication may be considered, also, as an acknowledgment of your letter of the 21st instant, in relation to the broken stone indicated.

Please make the necessary demands upon the contractor in accordance herewith.

Respectfully,

Supervising Architect.

Denver Mint, New.

Washington, D.C.,

December 21, 1901.

To the Supervising Architect,

Treasury Department.

Sir:

Complying with instructions contained in Departmental letter of Dec. 3, 1901, to make separate report of general inspection of Steel Work and certain other matters in the New Mint at Denver, Colorado, I have the honor to so report.

STEEL WORK.

The steel work except roof construction and tops of floor beams, is entirely enclosed in fireproofing. The steel work of roof was executed in strict accordance with the requirements of the specification and is a first-class piece of work - well painted and everything snug and well finished. Judging by this and the statements of Superintendent I am satisfied that the structural steel work of entire building was well erected. The paint has been entirely worn off the tops of floor beams and consequently a requirement is inserted in the interior finish specifications for re-painting same.

TERRA COTTA WORK.

The terra cotta was well set throughout the building , but owing to the defects afterward appearing due to exposure to the weather before building was roofed, a good deal of the floor work has been condemned by Superintendent. The disintegrated blocks in great numbers have been removed until in some rooms, the floors resemble a big sieve with perhaps 25 per cent of the terra cotta removed, the holes being of many shapes and sizes. Contractor is permitted to patch these floors on account of great expense of furnishing all new terra cotta, he taking the risk of floors standing the tests specified. Superintendent would have been fully justified in requiring the removal of entire sections of floor construction.

In the matter of marking the terra cotta for removal, Superintendent instead of being harsh has been liberal with contractor. Superintendent punches a hole in the soffit of every block to be removed throughout the floors. I examined some sections of floor thus spotted but where the terra cotta had not yet been removed and saw no blocks unfairly spotted. The terra cotta rejected can be easily crumbled in the fingers and is generally covered by a thick coat of efflorescence. The interior of the terra cotta substance also in many cases contained par-

icles of a white substance which I believe must have been the
source of the efflorescence. The work of repairing floors was
at a standstill during my visit.

BROKEN GLASS IN SKYLIGHT.

I examined the skylight construction and took up some of
the caps to see if glass was set too tight as claimed by contractor in his letter enclosed in letter of Superintendent, dated Nov. 19, 1901. I found no glass set too snug for expansion
hence I judge Superintendent made no unfair requirements during
construction. If any glass was set too snug it must have escap-
ed Superintendent's inspection. I am inclined to think the
glass which has cracked was not properly annealed. There is
very little of this broken glass and I recommend contractor be
required to replace same to satisfaction of Superintendent.

BROKEN STONES IN FACING OF BUILDING.

I examined the 5 broken stones mentioned in Superintendent's letter of Dec. 3, 1901, and also two others discovered
since that time and which have been or will be the subject of
another letter from Superintendent.

In view of the great difficulty of removing the stones,

I concur in Superintendent's recommendation that the contractor
be permitted to grout all the cracks with the special cement
noted except the stone "A-7-W-" and the cracked marble in upper
portion of one of rear windows, which are so broken that grout-
ing might not prove effective. Instead of removing the large
stone "A-7-W" as recommended in Superintendent's letter, I respectfully recommend that the broken portion of the stone be removed and a new piece be tenoned in as shown by accompanying
sketch. The cracked marble in one of the rear windows will form
the subject of a letter and sketch from Superintendent.

CRACKED TILE IN ROOF.

I examined the tile of roof mentioned in Superintendent's
letter of Nov. 19, 1901, and have to state that in my opinion
contractor is not responsible for the cracks mentioned. The tile
was solidly bedded in and pointed with Portland Cement mortar
as required. The tile approved and used was not the form shown
on drawings. It is too weak to stand much pressure sideways and
in such a large roof there must be expansion and contraction of
framework, and also of the tile itself. I am inclined to think
had elastic cement been used for pointing, as recommended by
tile-makers and the hard unyielding bed of Portland Cement been

4

omitted the cracks might not have appeared. I therefore respectfully recommend that the repairs to tiling be included in the
contract for interior finish, etc.

During my examination in connection with the proposed
interior modifications, the whole building was quite thoroughly
examined one story each day of my stay and I was impressed with
the general good workmanship obtained. It is much to be regret-
ted that the modifications to be made will necessarily impair
the work, especially the bonding of partition work and fireproofing which was particularly well done.

If the suggestions noted on drawings are adopted, some
of the most objectionable modifications will be avoided.

Respectfully submitted,

H.L. Averill

Structural Engineer.

EC 23 1901

P. J. AVERILL, etc.

Dec. 21, 1901.

Report on Floors, Broken
Stone, Glass, Tile, etc.

If the observations noted on drawings are adopted, much expensive and unsatisfactory modifications will be avoided.

Respectfully submitted,

[signature]

JOHN A. McINTYRE,
GENERAL CONTRACTOR.
Rooms 402-404 Cooper Building.
DENVER, COLO.
TELEPHONE 1228.

OWNER AND OPERATOR
ARKINS GRANITE QUARRIES.

Denver, Colo.,Jan. 31, 1902.

Lee Ullery, Esq.,

    Supt. Construction,

      New Mint, Denver.

Sir :

    I have the honor to acknowledge receipt of your letter of
Jany 29, 1902, advising me that the Treasury Department will make
the matter of cracked Spanish tile a part of a subsequent contract
for work on said building.

           Very Respectfully,

Denver, Colo., Jan.31,1902.

Lee Ullery,Esq.,

     Superintendent of Construction, New Mint, Denver.

:-

    Referring to your letter of Jan.29,1902, containing a suggestion as to the method of repairing stones A7W and A24S in said building together with certain other stones therein specifically mentioned and calling upon me for a definite statement of the amount I am willing to deduct from the amounts to be paid me, if I am permitted to re-pair the breaks in said stones in lieu of substituting new stone therefor, I have the honor to say:

    I have had the stones A7W and A24S carefully examined by a practical stone man, and am informed that the method suggested in your said letter will not secure as permanent and satisfactory result as the method I have the honor to hereby suggest.

    I will repair the breaks in the stones Q12E, L16E, A7W and A24S by thoroughly filling the fracture in each case with cement (to be duly approved) as was done in stone P14E, guaranteeing a permanent and satisfactory result in each case, and will repair the broken marble block over south second story window by removing the moulded portion and substituting new marble matching in material and finish with joint along the angle of the moulding,with similar guarantee to that given in case of broken granite.

;o deduct from the amounts still due me under my contract with the
United States,dated March 29,1898, for the Foundation,Superstructure
and Roof covering of the United States Mint building, the sum of Fifty Dollars.

                    Very Respectfully,
                          (Signed) J.A.McIntyre,
                                By Geo.E.Ross-Lewin, Atty.
                                                    T

to deduct from the amounts still due me under my contract with the United States, dated March 29, 1898, for the Foundation, Superstructure and Roof covering of the United States Mint building, the sum of Fifty Dollars.

Very Respectfully,

(Signed) J.A.McIntyre,

By Geo.E.Ross-Lewin, Atty.
T

DENVER, NEW MINT

LHB

*In replying to this Letter the
initials in upper right-hand
corner must be referred to.*

TREASURY DEPARTMENT

OFFICE OF THE SECRETARY

Washington, Jan. 28, 1902.

The Superintendent of Construction,
    New Mint,
        Denver, Colo.

Sir:

    Referring further to the matter of the desire of Mr. Harlow
and others that this Department recommend to Congress the granting
of a special appropriation for paving the streets about the Mint
building under your superintendency, you are advised that this Department does not feel that it can properly take the action requested.

        Respectfully,

                            Assistant Secretary.

JAW

T

Treasury Department,

The Superintendent of Construction,

    U. S. Mint Building, (New),

        Denver, Colorado.

Sir:

    In view of the request and recommendation contained in your letter of the 28th ultimo, and the public exigency requiring the immediate delivery of the articles and performance of the work you are hereby authorized to incur an expenditure of nine dollars ($9.00)

in securing in open market at lowest prevailing rates:

two tons of coal (2240 lbs., each,) for use in office of Superintendent, at $4.50 per ton, $ 9.00

    Your attention is called to printed "Instructions to Superintendents," and you will issue and certify vouchers on account of the above in accordance therewith, payment to be made from the appropriation for "Mint Building, Denver, Colo."

        Respectfully,

B.

                        Chief Executive Officer.

Form No. 108.

THE WESTERN UNION TELEGRAPH COMPANY.
——— INCORPORATED ———
21,000 OFFICES IN AMERICA.   CABLE SERVICE TO ALL THE WORLD.

This Company TRANSMITS and DELIVERS messages only on conditions limiting its liability, which have been assented to by the sender of the following message.
Errors can be guarded against only by repeating a message back to the sending station for comparison, and the Company will not hold itself liable for errors or delays
in transmission or delivery of Unrepeated Messages, beyond the amount of tolls paid thereon, nor in any case where the claim is not presented in writing within sixty days
after the message is filed with the Company for transmission.
This is an UNREPEATED MESSAGE, and is delivered by request of the sender, under the conditions named above.
THOS. T. ECKERT, President and General Manager.

/ 38

RECEIVED at 1114 to 1116 17th St., Denver, Colo.   NEVER CLOSED.

366

34 A MH NR 21 Pd Govt

Washington DC Feb. 12

Supt New Mint, Building Denver, Col.

Contractors proposal fifty dollars deduction repairing stones

accepted tenth instant.

J. K. Taylor.

Supervising Architect

9:50 a.m.

DENVER, NEW MINT.

TREASURY DEPARTMENT,

OFFICE OF THE SUPERVISING ARCHITECT,

Washington, February 8, 1902.

Superintendent of Construction,

    Mint Building,

        Denver, Colorado.

Sir:

    Referring to the Disbursing Agent's account for the month
of January, 1902, I have to call your attention to the fact
that you are required to brief all vouchers issued by you in
accordance with the forms before presenting them to the Disbursing Agent for payment.

                  Respectfully,

                        Chief Executive Officer.

FAB

DENVER NEW MINT.

TREASURY DEPARTMENT,

Enclosure 7056, OFFICE OF THE SUPERVISING ARCHITECT,

*In replying to this Letter the
initials in upper right-hand
corner must be referred to.*

Washington, Feb.10,1902.

Superintendent of Construction,
  New- Mint Building,
   Denver,Colorado.

Sir:-

  I enclose herewith, for your information and the files of
your office, a copy of Department letter of even date,accepting
the proposal of John A.McIntyre,the contractor for the foundation, superstructure and roof covering of the building in your
charge, to deduct the sum of fifty dollars ($50.00) from the
amount to be paid him under his contract, on account of making
necessary repairs to certain stones,-in lieu of furnishing new
stones,- and repairing two second story window sills, all as
stated in the said letter of acceptance.

  The Disbursing Agent has been advised of this deduction.

          Respectfully,

JSS

           Supervising Architect.

DENVER NEW MINT.

Feb.12,1902.

Mr. John A.McIntyre,
        Cooper Building,
            Denver,Colorado.

SIR:-

In view of the statement and recommendation contained in letter of the 21st ultimo from the Superintendent of Construction
of the New Mint at Denver,Colorado, your proposal,therein enclosed,
in accordance with the approval of this Department is hereby accepted to repair certain stones--named in your proposal-- in lieu
of furnishing new stones, in accordance with the terms of your
proposal and the Superintendent's letter to you of January 29,
1902,and to deduct the sum of fifty dollars ($50.00)-on account
thereof- from the amount to be paid you under your contract dated
March 29,1899 for the foundation,superstructure and roof covering
of the said building, it being a condition of this acceptance
that you are to make the necessary repairs to two second story
window sills, all to the entire satisfaction of the Superintendent,
a public exigency requiring this action.

It is understood and agreed that this deduction is not to affect the time for the completion of the work as required by the
terms of your contract; that the same is without prejudice to any
and all rights of the United States thereunder,and without prejudice,also, to any and all rights of the United States against the
sureties on the bond executed for the faithful fulfillment of the
contract.

DENVER NEW MINT, Feb. 10, 1902.
John A. McIntyre.

PAGE R.

Please promptly acknowledge the receipt of this letter, a copy
of which will be forwarded to the Superintendent of the building,
for his information.

                              Respectfully,

                                   Assistant Secretary.

Denver,Colo.,February 17,1902.

Honorable J.K.Taylor,

   Supervising Architect, Treasury Department,

   Washington, D.C.

Sir:-

   Having nearly completed work on the U.S.Mint
building,in this city, I have given up my office in the
Cooper Block and will therefore be pleased if you will direct all communications regarding said Mint to me at the
First National Bank, Denver, Colorado.

     Respectfully yours,

      (Signed) G.E.Ross-Lewin,Atty.,

      For John A.McIntyre.

Denver, Colo., February 17,1902.

Mr.Lee Ullery,

      Superintendent of Construction, U.S.Mint,

        Denver, Colorado.

Dear Sir:-

      I have this day requested the Department to forward
official communications in relation to the work on the U.S.Mint
building,in this city,directly to me at the First National Bank,
this city,having given up my office in the Cooper Block; and I
will be pleased if you will send all communications from your-
self regarding said work to me at the same address or deliver
them to my representative,Mr.Scott Truxtun.

           Respectfully yours,

                [signature] Atty

              for John A. McIntyre

DENVER. New Mint.

TREASURY DEPARTMENT,

OFFICE OF THE SUPERVISING ARCHITECT

Washington, February 17,1902.

143

Superintendent of Construction,

    U.S.Mint (New),

        Denver, Colorado.

Sir:

    Your letter of the 12th instant is acknowledged, reporting the
early completion of all work under contract with J.A.McIntyre, for the
erection of the superstructure, &c., at the building under your charge,
and in reply, you are advised that in view of the recent inspection
made of the building, it is not deemed necessary to make another examination of the work, and you are therefore requested, when entire completion has been secured, to report in line with Section XL of printed
"Instructions to Superintendents".

           Respectfully,

                    Supervising Architect.

TO SUPERINTENDENTS OF CONSTRUCTION OF PUBLIC BUILDINGS.

-------------oOo-------------

The accompanying forms of vouchers will hereafter be used to the exclusion of all other forms now in stock when issuing and certifying vouchers for payments accruing under formal contracts on account of construction operations, and also for the payment of open market authorizations under public exigency. The long form of voucher, for payments under contract, should only be used when it is found that the shorter form, by reason of the details to be inserted, cannot be made to answer.

Superintendents must fill out the briefing (with the exception of the number) on the backs of all vouchers prior to their presentation for payment. The number will be filled in by the Disbursing Agent, or at the Department, as the case may be.

The title of the appropriation, which is to be inserted at the top of the voucher, on the lines reserved for that purpose, and also in the briefing on the back, must accord, word for word, with the title as it is quoted in the letters of authorization from the Department.

With the exhaustion of the forms sent herewith, requisition should be made on this office for an additional supply.

James Knox Taylor,

Supervising Architect.

Washington, D.C.,
February 17, 1902.

Form No. 184.
24 V.29 1901 1,000.

NOTICE TO SUPERINTENDENT THAT NO FUNDS WILL BE REMITTED TO DISBURSING AGENT.

Treasury Department,

OFFICE OF THE SUPERVISING ARCHITECT,

Washington, D. C.,

Superintendent *Mint Building*
Denver, Colorado.

Sir:

I have to acknowledge the receipt of your Estimate of Funds required for the work on the building under your superintendence during the month of *February* , 190*2*, and to advise you that, as it appears the remittance of funds heretofore made to the Disbursing Agent is sufficient to meet all vouchers issued or to be issued for expenditures on account of the work, to and including the last day of the current month, no further remittance will be made to him at present.

Respectfully,

Chief Executive Officer.

Form No. 184.
Ed. 8 29 1901 1,000.

NOTICE TO SUPERINTENDENT THAT NO FUNDS WILL BE REMITTED TO DISBURSING AGENT.

Treasury Department,

OFFICE OF THE SUPERVISING ARCHITECT,

Washington, D. C.,

Superintendent

Mint Building,
Denver, Colorado.

Sir:

I have to acknowledge the receipt of your Estimate of Funds required for the work on the building under your superintendence during the month of *February* , 190*2*, and to advise you that, as it appears the remittance of funds heretofore made to the Disbursing Agent is sufficient to meet all vouchers issued or to be issued for expenditures on account of the work, to and including the last day of the current month, no further remittance will be made to him at present.

Respectfully,

Chief Executive Officer.

Denver,Colo.,March 4,1902.

Honorable J.K.Taylor,
    Supervising Architect,
      Washington, D.C.

Sir:-

      Having in June,1899, assumed all obligations of J.A.Mc-tyre under his contract dated March 29,1898, for the Foundation, Superstructure and Roof-covering of the United States Mint Building Denver, Colorado, and desiring final payment in accordance with the terms of said contract, I now tender to the United States the said building for inspection and acceptance.

      Referring to the guarantee of "The entire roof covering, including all tiling, copper work, skylight and drainage therefor", called for and required on page "B-3" of the specifications for said building, I have the honor to say,-

      I will carry out and make effective said guarantee for the period of one year in so far as the same refers to the "copper work" and drainage therefor". I will for the same length of time guarantee "all tiling" from any inherent defects of material, saving and excepting only all cracks caused by contraction and expansion or by the methods of construction called for in the plans and specifications. In so far as the skylight proper is concerned, I have the honor to say, that although the greatest care was exercised and the plans and specifications duly and carefully complied with, said skylight does and always has leaked, although the same has been carefully and repeatedly inspected by your Superintendent of Construction and his suggestions regarding the same in all instances carefully carried out. I believe that the leaks referred to are due to some defects in the method of construction called for and not in any way chargeable to the contractor, and I therefore request that I be relieved from a guarantee in respect to the same except as to materials and workmanship, any defects in which I will remedy promptly when notified of the same.

      WITNESS my hand and seal, this fourth day of March, A.D. 1902.

                (Signed) G.E.Ross-Lewin (Seal)

Scott Truxtun,   Witness,
W.C.Smith,   Witness.

U. S. Court House and Post Office

Pueblo,Colo,Mch 12,1902.

Mr.Lee Ullery

Superintendent of Construction,U.S.Mint,

Denver,Colo.

Dear Sir:

Following is copy of telegram received by me;-

Washington,D.C. Mch 10,1902.

Letter mailed today accepting Piper Bros. bid for revolving doors.

Signed, J.K.Taylor, Supervising Architect.

The bid of Piper Bros. is in the sum of $2375.00,and is based upon Drawing #142,and the specifications originally prepared.

I have heard nothing whatever from the Department relative to repairs,painting,etc.,as per specifications prepared by you last year. Have you heard anything concerning the same?

I will be pleased to receive any suggestions you care to make.

Very respectfully,

Custodian.

Form No. 184.
Ed. 8 29 1901 1,000.

NOTICE TO SUPERINTENDENT THAT NO FUNDS WILL BE REMITTED TO DISBURSING AGENT.

Treasury Department,

OFFICE OF THE SUPERVISING ARCHITECT,

Washington, D. C., *March 13, 1902,*

Superintendent *Mint Building,*
Denver, Colo.

Sir:

I have to acknowledge the receipt of your Estimate of Funds required for the work on the building under your superintendence during the month of *February* , 190*2*, and to advise you that, as it appears the remittance of funds heretofore made to the Disbursing Agent is sufficient to meet all vouchers issued or to be issued for expenditures on account of the work, to and including the last day of the current month, no further remittance will be made to him at present.

Respectfully,

Seymour

Chief Executive Officer.

DENVER NEW MINT.

In replying to this Letter the initials in upper right-hand corner must be referred to.

TREASURY DEPARTMENT,

OFFICE OF THE SUPERVISING ARCHITECT

Washington, March 14, 1902.

Superintendent of Construction,
New Mint Building,
Denver, Colorado.

Sir:

I have to acknowledge the receipt of your letter of the 10th instant, containing information relative to Red Diamond Portland cement used in connection with the contract of Mr. J.A.McIntyre for the foundation, superstructure,etc., of the building in your charge and in which you also state that you desire instructions as to the necessity of again requiring the contractor to patch certain work, and you are advised that it is the opinion of this Office that any work which is to be done in the future should not affect the responsibility of the present contractor to leave his work in perfect condition and if, through fault of his, the covering is not what the contract requires it to be, he should be directed to make it good.

What you say relative to the use of imported Portland cement for future exterior work, has been noted but the experience of this Office with the best brands of American Portland cement has been so satisfactory that it is not deemed wise to bar it, however, after the experience with Red Diamond cement it will probably be considered inexpedient to permit that brand to be used for such purposes.

Respectfully,

Supervising Architect.

WFR

(PRINTED COPY).

Denver,Colo.,March 21,1902.

Mr.C.E.Kemper,
    Chief Executive Officer U.S.Treasury,
     Washington, D.C.

S I R :
    Referring to your letter "P" March 15,1902, requesting a
statement as to cause of the failure to complete the United States
Mint building(New) in this city under my contract with the United
States, dated March 29,1898,within the time called for in said contract,under an obligation to forfeit as liquidated damages the sum
of Twenty Dollars ($20.00) per day for each day's delay not caused
by the Government, I have the honor to say said delay was caused,

    I. By the change from Cotopaxi to Arkins Granite quarries and
the unforseen difficulties attending the opening of said Arkins quarries, no quarring for building purposes having been done heretofore
in that locality.

    II. Delay caused by change from Colorado marble as called for
in the specifications to Tennessee marble, much delay having been
experienced in securing material acceptable to the United States, and
after the acceptance of the same the closing of the Tennessee River
for over thirty (30) days by order of R.R.Thatcher, United States
River Inspector.

    III. The delay caused by going to Maine for the top member of
the granite cornice, which delay prevented the completion of the
walls and roofing of said building exposing the terra cotta in place
to the effects of weather, thereby greatly damaging same and causing
several months extra work thereon.

    IV. Delay caused by bad and freezing weather during the year
1899 when exceptionally severe weather was encountered preventing
all work at the quarry for a considerable length of time.

    V. And further delays caused from time to time by circumstan-
ces either unforseen and beyond the control of the contractor,each
of which caused a greater or less loss of time, amounting to a considerable period of time in the aggregate.

    In view of the fact that the above delays were entailed
by causes entirely unforseen and impossible to guard against and
therefore not chargeable to neglect or carelessness upon my part and
the further fact that I had trusted the delay attendant upon the
completing of my contract which so far has worked the Government no
actual damage, I have the honor to ask that said forfeiture be not
enforced against me.

    I have the honor to request that all mail in regard to the
Mint matter be forwarded me in care of the First National Bank,Den-
ver, Colorado.
                Very respectfully,
                  (Signed) John A.McIntyre,
                  By C.D.Ross-Lewin,Atty.

DENVER, NEW MINT.

In replying to this Letter the initials in upper right-hand corner must be referred to.

TREASURY DEPARTMENT
OFFICE OF THE SUPERVISING ARCHITECT

Washington, **March 21,1902.**

/65 /

3

Superintendent of Construction,

U.S.Mint (New),

Denver, Colorado.

Sir:

Your letter of the 17th instant is hereby acknowledged, and in view of the statements therein made, you are advised that it is not deemed necessary to take photographs of the building under your charge at the end of the present month.

Respectfully,

Supervising Architect.

PUFBIO.

B

Inclosure No. 7180.

Mr. Lee Ullery,

    Superintendent of Construction,

        U. S. Mint,

            Denver, Colorado.

Sir:

    There are inclosed herewith three (3) copies of specification prepared from your reports of November 13th and 15th, 1901, for repairs, painting, etc., at the Post Office, Pueblo, Colorado, for which the Custodian of the building named has been this day authorized to advertise for proposals.

    You are requested to immediately communicate with the Custodian at Pueblo for the purpose of ascertaining the date fixed for opening proposals, and to then confer with contractors in your city with a view to securing proposals from them for the performance of the work, said proposals to be forwarded to and opened by the Custodian at Pueblo.

               Respectfully,

                    Acting Supervising Architect.

U. S. Court House and Post Office

Pueblo,Colo,Mch 28,1902.

Mr.Lee Ullery

Supt.of Construction,U.S.Mint,

Denver,Colo.

Dear Sir:-

Referring to your two letters of the 27th inst.,
relative to repairs,painting,etc.,at this building,I beg to advise
that I have set the 28th day of April,at 2 o'clock,P.M. as a date
for opening proposals for said work. The changes in specification
at page 8,as suggested by you have been made in the eight copies
sent me. Thanking you for any suggestions you may see fit to
make,and for any assistance in the matter,I am

Very respectfully,

Custodian.

Form No. 60.
Ed. 7 28 1901 5,000.

DENVER, NEW MINT
AUTHORITY FOR OPEN-MARKET PURCHASE.
(All letters in reply to official communications must refer to control in upper right-hand corner)

Treasury Department,

OFFICE OF THE SUPERVISING ARCHITECT.

Washington, D. C., March 26, 1902.

The Superintendent of Construction,

Mint Building, (new),

Denver, Colorado.

Sir:

In view of the request and recommendation contained in your letter of the 17th instant and the public exigency requiring the immediate delivery of the articles and performance of the work you are hereby authorized to incur an expenditure of eight dollars and sixty cents ($8.60)

in securing in open market at lowest prevailing rates:

twenty (20) gallons of coal oil for use of watchman $ 3.60

     repairs to office structure,   5.00

Your attention is called to printed "Instructions to Superintendents," and you will issue and certify vouchers on account of the above in accordance therewith, payment to be made from the appropriation for "Mint Building, Denver, Col."

Respectfully,

Acting Chief Executive Officer

TREASURY DEPARTMENT

OFFICE OF THE SECRETARY

Washington, March 29,1902.

The Superintendent of Construction,

    U. S. Mint Building,

        Denver, Colorado.

Sir:

    Referring to your letter of the 17th instant, addressed
to the Supervising Architect and referred to this office, you
are informed that one National Ensign 4 1/4 x 8 feet, for use
of the new Mint Building at Denver, has been forwarded by to-
day's mail to your address.

    You are requested to acknowledge the receipt of same.

                Respectfully,

                           Captain, R.C.S.,
                          Chief of Division.
                          S

DENVER NEW MINT.

The Superintendent of Construction,

   United States (new) Mint,

      Denver, Colorado.

Sir:

   The receipt of your letter of the 27th ultimo
relative to the leaks in the skylight of the building for which you are the Superintendent of Construction is hereby acknowledged,and in reply you
are advised that it is not considered advisable to
include this work in the interior finish contract.

   A drawing showing the necessary changes will,
however,be prepared and forwarded as soon as possible,in order that a proposal may be obtained
therefor.

      Respectfully,

                        Supervising Architect.

   R.

DENVER. MINT. (NEW).

S.H.

TREASURY DEPARTMENT,

OFFICE OF THE SUPERVISING ARCHITECT,

Washington, **April 4, 1902.**

Enclosure 8568.

Superintendent of Construction,

    Mint, (New),

        Denver, Colorado.

Sir:

    In reply to your inquiry of the 24th ultimo, you are informed that this office does not anticipate any obstacles to your taking your leave as requested. It is suggested that you send in your formal application for leave about the first of the coming month when the matter will receive due consideration.

    The two cent stamp which accompanied your letter is herewith returned.

               Respectfully,

                       Supervising Architect.

DENVER, NEW MINT

In replying to this Letter the
initials in upper righthand
corner must be referred to.

TREASURY DEPARTMENT,

OFFICE OF THE SUPERVISING ARCHITECT,

Washington,   April 7, 1902.

Superintendent of Construction,

      Mint Building,

           Denver, Colorado.

Sir:-

      Your attention is called to the fact that you quote
the appropriation, on vouchers issued by you for expenditures
against the building in your charge, as "U. S. Mint Building,
Denver, Colo." The correct title of this appropriation, and
the one which you must use, is "Mint Building, Denver, Colo."
In the future preparation of vouchers, it is requested that
you omit the use of the initials "U. S!, as the Departmental
requirement necessitates the quoting of appropriations literally
in order to conform to statutory provisions.

      Respectfully,

              Acting Chief Executive Officer.

FD

DENVER, NEW MINT

1 5 (

TREASURY DEPARTMENT,

OFFICE OF THE SUPERVISING ARCHITECT,

Washington, **April 8, 1902.**

Superintendent of Construction,

      Mint Building,

         Denver, Colorado.

Sir:-

    I have to advise you that a request has this day
been made for a remittance to the Disbursing Agent of the
building in your charge, in the sum of............$25,000.00,
on account of the appropriation for "Mint Building, Denver,
Colorado," to enable him to make payment of authorized expenditures.

      Respectfully,

        Jas. A. Wenderoth

        Acting Chief Executive Officer.

FD

Washington, April __, ____

ies,

irposed the provision stipulating the
ed damages for delay in completion of
ct with John A.McIntyre of Denver,
superstructure and roof covering of
Colorado, only in so far as to charge
actual cost to the United States of
force at the building for the last
lation of the entire work, amounting
by directed to prepare, certify and
the contractor, in the sum
...............................$13,889.80,
ing under said contract and proposals
in addition thereto, after making the
the voucher in question to be paid
the building named, from funds in

r, Colorado."

The following is a statement of the account:-

Contract accepted   Foundation, Superstructure
  March 29, 1898.   and Roof Covering.........$247,874.09

Proposal accepted Oct. 20, 1898......$ 85.00
    "   "   "   21, " 2,027.00
    "   "   Feb. 6, 1900......   40.00
    "   "   Sep. 22, " 20.00
    "   "   Dec. 13, " 20.00
    "   "   "   14, " 500.00
    "   "   Mar. 29, 1901......   25.00
    "   "   Apr. 16, " 35.00
    "   "   June 19, " 10.00   2,762.00
                                                     250,636.09
    Less deduction Apr. 24, 1901......$ 4.00
      "   "   June 29, " 175.00
      "   "   Sept. 9, " 50.00
      "   "   Feb. 10, 1902...... 50.00   279.00
                                                     250,357.09
    Less payments on account.................... 225,366.38
                                                      24,990.71
    Less actual cost to Government to maintain
      contingent force at building during last
      18 months prior to completion of work..... 10,601.21
                      Amount of proposed voucher........ 14,389.50

                      Respectfully,

                      Jas. A. Erdman
                      Acting Chief Executive Officer.

FAB.

DENVER NEW MINT.

TREASURY DEPARTMENT,

OFFICE OF THE SUPERVISING ARCHITECT

Washington,   April 26, 1902.

ENCLOSURE 4363.
FORWARDING.

The Superintendent of Construction,
     New Mint Building,
         Denver, Colorado.

Sir:-

     I enclose herewith advertisement, and Authorities dated
March 21, 1902, for its insertion in the "Republican" and "Times",
daily, and "Western Construction", weekly, newspapers of your city,
inviting proposals for the completion (except certain steel vaults,
plumbing, elevators, heating apparatus, electric wiring and conduits)
of the building in your charge. Please have the advertisement pub-
lished as required by the Authorities.

     There are forwarded, under separate cover, six (6) sets of
the drawings and specifications for this work, one for the files
of your office and the others for the use of competent parties who
may desire to submit proposals.

     You are requested to keep this Office advised as to the par-
ties to whom you furnish plans and specifications, in order that
duplicate sets may not be sent them, and as soon as the bids are
opened to collect and return to this Office all drawings and specifications sent you, except one set to be retained for the files of
your office.

                Respectfully,

                                   Chief Executive Officer.

INCLOSURE 4363.
FORWARDING.

The Superintendent of Construction,
        New Mint Building,
                Denver, Colorado.
    Sir:-

        I enclose herewith advertisement, and Authorities dated
March 21, 1902, for its insertion in the "Republican" and "Times",
daily, and "Western Construction", weekly, newspapers of your city,
inviting proposals for the completion (except certain steel vaults,
plumbing, elevators, heating apparatus, electric wiring and conduits)
of the building in your charge. Please have the advertisement pub-
lished as required by the Authorities.

        There are forwarded, under separate cover, six (6) sets of
the drawings and specifications for this work, one for the files
of your office and the others for the use of competent parties who
may desire to submit proposals.

        You are requested to keep this Office advised as to the par-
ties to whom you furnish plans and specifications, in order that
duplicate sets may not be sent them, and as soon as the bids are
opened to collect and return to this Office all drawings and specifications sent you, except one set to be retained for the files of
your office.

                    Respectfully,

                            _____
                            Chief Executive Officer.

Lee Ullery,

    Sup't of Construction U.S.(new) Mint,

        Denver, Colorado.

Dear Sir:--

    I beg to acknowledge the receipt this day of package from you containing the ground floor plan of this building.

    As you may be interested in learning the result of the examination of bids for repairs, opened yesterday, I give you the following figures:

    Piper Bros., $8,958.00.

    Campbell & Richardson, $9,085.00.

    Martin J. Wicklem, $9,463.00.

                Respectfully,

                        Custodian.

L. S. GILLETTE, PRESIDENT.
G. M. GILLETTE, SEC. & TREAS.

A. Y. BAYNE, MGR. BRIDGE DEPT

THE GILLETTE-HERZOG MANUFACTURING COMPANY.

OFFICES 1008 TO 1012 GUARANTY BUILDING.

163

MINNEAPOLIS, MINN.

May 2nd, 1902.

Mr. Lee Ullery, Supt.,

U. S. Mint,

Denver, Col.

Dear Sir:-

I have this morning yours of the 30th ult. stating that the gates cannot now be used and the reason for the change. Of course I am greatly disappointed but just the same we all fully appreciate your kindness and care in the case. Such things will happen in spite of all one can do.

May I trouble you a little about the man-hole covers and frames about which you wrote me some time ago? Will they be used and if so is there anything in it for the Company in them? I have no idea how many there are nor the value. I dislike to trouble you about these matters Mr. Ullery, but I don't see any other way to do.

Again thanking you for all your kindness and attention to our interests, we are,

Very truly yours,

THE GILLETTE-HERZOG MFG.CO.

By

The Piper Bros Co. **BUILDERS** INCORPORATED

OFFICE
220 W SECOND ST.
P.O. BOX 3

PUEBLO, COLO. May 8th. _____ 190 2

Lee Ullery,

       Supt. Construction, U.S.Mint,

           Denver,Colo.

Dear Sir:- -

       On April 28th. we made a proposal to the Department for certain repairs, alterations and changes to be made in the U.S.Post Office Building, this City. The Supervising Architect desires to omit certain items; we would like to have you explain in this connection a little more fully what you mean about changes in the skylight screens.

       You say in your specifications as follows:

       "The glass in the skylight to be removed and the wire screens now in place are to be lowered and secured in place and the beams and channels immediately beneath the sash bars with angles, plates, etc. bolted to the screen framing; the 4 inch leg of angle to rest on the channels and the 2 inch leg to stand vertical and to rest against the beam or channel and all the screens to be held in place secure."

       We understand that these screens when they are lowered have to be cut off, made shorter so as to go between the beams or channels as the case may be, lowering perhaps 4 inches, from their present position.

       See sketch.

Are we correct in this supposition? Is the angle mentioned a con-
inuous angle or is it a lug ?

A reply by return mail will greatly oblige,

Yours respectfully,

The Pieper Bros Co

DIVISION OF STATIONERY, PRINTING, AND BLANKS. }
Form No. 82.—Ed. 9 15 1900 1,000. }

Treasury Department,

OFFICE OF THE SECRETARY.

May 2 ...., 190 2

Sir:

Your requisition of ....May..6........., 190 2, for stationery
has been received, and will be filled as soon as possible. It must be
borne in mind that the Public Printer requires two months' time in
which to print paper and envelopes.

Respectfully,

Geo. Simpson

Chief of Division of Stationery, Printing, and Blanks.

Per S

NOTICE TO SUPERINTENDENT THAT NO FUNDS WILL BE REMITTED TO DISBURSING AGENT.

Treasury Department,

OFFICE OF THE SUPERVISING ARCHITECT.

Washington, D. C., May 10, 1902.

Superintendent of Construction,
        Mint Building,
            Denver, Colo.

Sir:

I have to acknowledge the receipt of your Estimate of Funds required for the work on the building under your superintendence during the month of   May   , 1902, and to advise you that, as it appears the remittance of funds heretofore made to the Disbursing Agent is sufficient to meet all vouchers issued or to be issued for expenditures on account of the work, to and including the last day of the current month, no further remittance will be made to him at present.

Respectfully,

[signature]

Chief Executive Officer.

F. A. PURDY
ARCHITECTURAL SCULPTOR
7820 BOND AVENUE
CARVING AND MODELING IN WOOD, STONE,
GRANITE, ETC.

TEMPORARY CITY OFFICE:
New Federal Building

CHICAGO, _May 14_ 1902

The Custodian of the Bennac Mine

Bennac, Ont.

Dear Sir

I learn that there is considerable
carving in marble yet to be done upon
the Mine in-Bennac. Would you kindly
inform me if this be so, and if it
will probably be placed under contract
this summer, as I wish to submit
a proposal for doing the work.

RECEIVED at 1114 to 1116 17th St., Denver, Colo.   754   NEVER CLOSED.

527

~~501~~ Ch. Wo. Q. 64 Paid. Gov't

Washington, D. C., May 15th, 1902.

Sup't New Mint Bldg,

Denver, Colo

This office is informed utica nonstaining cement was used in
following buildings in your city in setting lime and sand-stone:
Equitable Life; Brown Palace Hotel; Boston Building; Denver Club;
Denver Athletic Club; Report by mail if such is the case
and whether you can recommend said cement for use in cheyenne
building.

                    Chas. E. Kemper, Acting Supervising Architect

4x5

~~345~~ Pm.

524 E. 134th St., NEW YORK, ...May 16, 1902.

C.F.

Superintendent, U.S.Mint,

Denver, Cele.

Dear Sir:

In cennection with the censtructien of the U.S.Mint at
Denver, we desire te present fer censideratien the advisability ef
using revolving doors at the entrances ef this building. These revelving doors, as you are ne doubt aware, keep out all snow, wind, rain and
dust, as well as preving ecenemical in fuel. They are being specified
by the Supervising Architect in all ef the new Pest Office buildings
and ne doubt sheuld alse be in your building.

We would be glad te have you send us a plan and elevatien ef the
entrance of the building se that we may submit drawing and prepesitien
fer furnishing revelving doors.

You will ne deubt, be able te save seme time in cerrespondence if
yeu will cemmunicate with eur western effice in the Chamber ef Cemmerce
building, Chicago, Ill.

Heping to hear from you seen, we remain,

Respectfully yours,

Van Kannel Revolving Door Co.

General Sales Manager

J.W.F.
JLN

DENVER NEW MINT.

ENCLOSURE 4380.

TREASURY DEPARTMENT,
OFFICE OF THE SUPERVISING ARCHITECT.

Washington, May 19, 1902.

The Superintendent of Construction,
    New Mint Building,
        Denver, Colorado.

Sir:-

    I enclose herewith advertisement, and Authorities dated May 15, 1902, for its insertion in the "Republican" and "Times", daily, and "Western Construction", weekly, newspapers of your city, inviting proposals for the mechanical equipment(except engines and generators) for the building in your charge. Please have the advertisement published as required by the Authorities.

    There will be forwarded to you within the next few days six (6) sets of the drawings and specifications for this work, one for the files of your office and the others for the use of competent parties who may desire to submit lump sum proposals for the entire work.

    You are requested to keep this Office advised as to the parties to whom you furnish plans and specifications, in order that duplicate sets may not be sent them, and as soon as the bids are opened to collect and return to this Office all drawings and specifications forwarded to you, except one set to be retained for your office files.

            Respectfully,

                                Chief Executive Officer.

J.G.

TREASURY DEPARTMENT,

OFFICE OF THE SUPERVISING ARCHITECT,

Washington, May 20, 1902.

Messrs. Forster & Smith,
  U.S.Public Building,
    Cheyenne,Wyoming.

Gentlemen:-

Referring to your telegram of the 14th instant,giving
the names of certain buildings in which you stated Utica containing cement was used in setting the stone, I have to advise you that
the buildings mentioned which are in Denver,Colorado have been
investigated and it has been found that while this brand of
cement was used in setting the brick and terra cotta of a portion of the buildings,there is no definite information that it
was used in setting the stone work;and in several of the buildings
it is reported not to have been used at all. Therefore the following telegram has been sent you this day, which is hereby confirmed:

"Investigation shows that Utica containing cement
was not used in majority of buildings referred
to by you,and the same is rejected.Letter."

Respectfully,

Supervising Architect.

JEa

CHEYENNE.

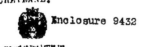Enclosure 9432

Superintendent of Construction,
New Mint Building,
Denver, Colorado.

Sir:-

I have to acknowledge the receipt of your letter of the 17th
instant, reporting upon the buildings in your City, mentioned in
telegram to you of the 15th instant, in which the contractors for
the construction of the U.S.Public Building at Cheyenne, Wyoming
claimed Utica nonstaining cement was used in setting the stone;
and to enclose herewith ,for your information, a copy of a letter
this day addressed to them in regard to the matter, which explains
itself.

                    Respectfully,

                              (Supervising Architect.

JSS

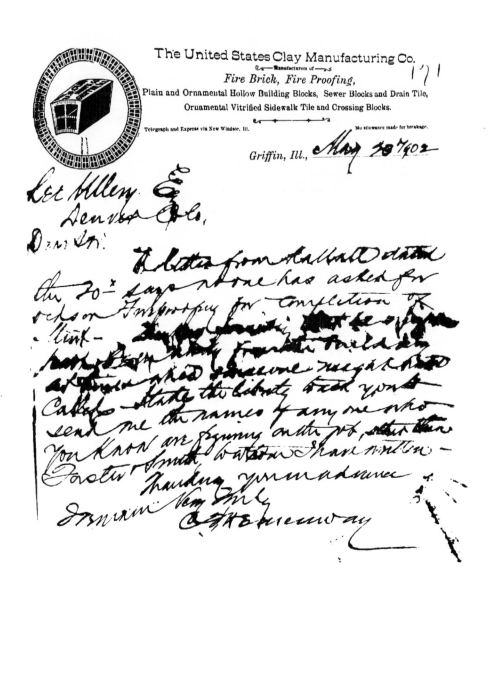

The United States Clay Manufacturing Co.

Manufacturers of

Fire Brick, Fire Proofing,

Plain and Ornamental Hollow Building Blocks, Sewer Blocks and Drain Tile,

Ornamental Vitrified Sidewalk Tile and Crossing Blocks.

Telegraph and Express via New Windsor, Ill.   No allowance made for breakage.

Griffin, Ill., *May 28 1902*

171

Lee Allen Esq.
    Denver Colo,

Dear Sir:

The letter from Hallock dated
the 20th says no one has asked for
bids on Fireproofing for completion of
Mint —

State the names of any one who
you know are figuring on the job,
Foster & Smith & Watson I have written —

Thanking you in advance

I remain Very truly

C. H. Hemenway

172

Supt U. S. Mint Building

Dear Sir,

I may conclude
to submit bid for Mint Building
and if you can consistantly answer
the following will thank you for it
What is the character of soil to be
excavated Is not Basement story
granite of Platte Canyon I understand
all arches of Fire Proofing are in
also all partitions except as indicated
on plans, About what are the prices
for 6" 4" x 2" tile partitions

I could not get out to Denver
to look it over I suppose all
the work is in pretty good shape
so far as frames and other
points Any other information
will be appreciated
Address me Washington City,
D. C. Care of Arlington Hotel
I am erecting a $750,000.00 office building
at Uniontown Pa — yours truly

James A. McGonigle

Chas. B. Kruse Heating Company,

CONTRACTORS FOR

POWER PLANTS, STEAM, HOT WATER
AND FAN HEATING,

And General Steam Fitting Promptly
Attended To.

117 West Water Street.
TELEPHONE MAIN 838.

Milwaukee, Wis. June 4th, 1907.

Superintendent of Construction,

U. S. Mint Bldg.,

Denver, Colorado.

Dear Sir;-

We expect to make a proposal for the Mechanical Equipment
of the Building under your charge, and if convenient to you, we would
thank you to let us know as soon as may be, what subcontractors we can
write to for prices on Plumbing, Switchboard, Electric Wiring & Conduit System, Electric Elevators & Pipe Covering. We expect you will
know what firms of your City are figuring on the above; hence, our
reason for addressing you. We would also like to know how far the
Building is advanced, and besides the above, we would like to know
who we could write to for prices, on Mason work, Galvanized Iron Work,
artesian well & Marble work.

If the above is going to inconvenience you too much then
answer only what you feel like answering, and very greatly,

Respectfully yours,

CHAS. B. KRUSE HEATING CO.,

Per Juttner.

Chief Executive Officer.

N
O
P
Q

Steingoetter, L. 82
Shoemaker. C. F. 3. 15.15
Schieren, Chas. A. & Co. 17

Index to letters from

Assistant Secretary

Supervising Architect

John A. McIntyre
G. E. Ross-Lewin

Assistant Secretary H. A. Taylor.

Visit Iron Mountain, Wyoming & examine quarries
 "   Ulm sandstone quarry, Montana
 "   Columbus "   "
 '   Pueblo Post Office
 "   .   "   " in re repairs, painting, storm doors
Report to Supervising Architect as to condition of Post Office, &c.
Visit Iron Mountain & Rawlins quarries, Wyo. — report
Telegram: Unnecessary to visit quarries. Return and report
Department cannot ask for appropriation for street paving
 .   "   "   "   "   "   "